DIGITAL
SURVIVAL
GUIDE

ROY CAMP

Edited by Stephanie Gorton Murphy
Book icons designed by Freepik

To protect the privacy of certain individuals the names and identifying details have been changed. The information contained within this book is for general guidance and strictly for educational and research purposes.

This publication is designed to provide accurate and authoritative information in regard to the subject matter covered but it is sold with the understanding that the author and publisher are not engaged in rendering legal, accounting, financial, business, technical, or other professional service. Laws vary from state to state and each situation may have individual requirements; if legal advice, any expert assistance, any technical, any financial, any accounting, any business, or any other assistance is required, the services of a competent professional should be sought as this publication is not a substitute for professional assistance and the reader should not rely on it as such.

The author and publisher specifically disclaim any liability for loss or risk, damage, disruption, personal or otherwise, which is incurred as a consequence, directly or indirectly, of the use and application of any of the contents of this book whether such loss is caused by errors or omissions, negligence, outdated content, or for any other reason.

Library of Congress Cataloging-in-Publication Data
    Names: Camp, Roy.
    Title: Digital Survival Guide / Roy Camp
    Description: pages cm. Includes bibliographical references and index.
    Identifiers: LCCN 2016930805 | ISBN 978-0-9972137-9-9 (pbk. book) |
    ISBN 9780997213782 (hardcover)
    LC record available at https://lccn.loc.gov/2016930805

Printed in the United States of America.

Books are available at quantity discounts for government, educational institutions and training programs. For information please visit the Contact page at https://digitalsurvivalguide.net

CONTENTS

INTRODUCTION

W<small>E LIVE</small> in a digital age. The communications revolution of the last two decades has transformed the way we communicate and learn about one another. Take a moment to think about all the people who might have Googled you at some point: admissions officers, hiring managers, and prospective dates, to name a few—never mind law enforcement, insurance underwriters, and less legitimate operators. Are you taking the necessary steps to keep your identity, privacy, and money safe?

Cyber crime is on the rise—and it is only going to continue to increase, both in frequency and severity. These are familiar stories: a friend's email account suddenly starts sending Spam messages, or a relative's credit card number was stolen, or you discover an ex who knows your password is reading your emails. Or you had to check that your email and financial details weren't compromised in a larger cyber attack, maybe after seeing headlines about privacy and security leaks at Sony, Target, Home Depot, eBay, or Anthem. In 2014, there was a new report of identity theft nearly every two seconds.[1] Have you done anything to protect against the inevitable theft or fraud that is attempted against you or your family?

With the increase in how connected our lives are, there seems to be an equal uptick in how busy we have become. Safety and security often come at the expense of convenience: it's a trade-off not many of us take seriously or prioritize until it's too late. But there are many straightforward, inexpensive, commonsense ways to customize your approach and find the balance that is right for you. Even a minimal investment of time and effort can significantly increase your level of security and peace of mind. That way, when you or your family is targeted, it will merely be a minor inconvenience—not a costly ordeal. That's where The Digital Survival Guide comes in: this book will give you the knowledge and tools you need to design a digital security plan that fits your life.

The Digital Survival Guide is designed to be concise and covers a broad spectrum of subjects — everything you need to know to protect yourself in the digital age. This book is geared toward the average individual who uses technology. If you consider yourself to be less than tech savvy, do not fear — I provide links to supplemental beginner material throughout the book. If you consider yourself to be a technology expert, you'll surely still find this book beneficial, and I have provided links to advanced supplemental material for you as well.

Icons used in this book

Remember

I don't expect you to remember everything in this book, but keep an eye out for this icon. It signals an essential concept that you'll want to keep in mind.

Tip

The tip icon signifies useful advice

Resource

I provide links throughout the book to products, services, and supplemental reading materials. For convenience, and because those resources will evolve and change alongside digital technologies, I link to them with handy shortened URL's that start with: http://dsg.tips/

Did you know?

These are facts and statistics about our digital age that will help form your security plan.

You are at risk

Have you thought about what the impact is that identity theft could have on you, your life, your family, even your career? Taking proactive steps to protect your identity, privacy, and money is usually an afterthought, despite all there is at stake. In 2014, 12.7 million Americans were victims of identity theft, with a total of over $16 billion stolen from victims. [2] That is equivalent to a new victim nearly every two seconds. An identity theft survey conducted by the FTC showed that victims spend an average of 30 to 60 hours and $500-$1,200 to repair their identity.[3] Not to mention the stress and inconvenience identity theft causes.

Did you know?

► The IRS tells victims it takes 180 days to resolve tax identity theft; however, it actually takes an average of 278 days. One out of every 10 cases is resolved incorrectly.[39]

Everyone is at risk, including children. In fact, kids are common targets for identity theft because their identities are a clean slate. Since it has never occurred to most parents that they need to take proactive steps to protect their children's identities, many young adults face a nasty surprise the first time they apply for credit or even lease an apartment.

It is important to protect yourself and your family – and your workplace shouldn't be left out, either. The largest digital security threat to any company, big or small, is you, the employee. Not because you have malicious intent, but rather because you inadvertently or naively opened an attachment you shouldn't have, provided your credentials to hackers, or provided some sort of confidential information by accident. If you work in any capacity in healthcare, government, education, police force, or a large company, you are at especially high risk of being targeted.

Much of this theft and fraud is never reported to the police. Because of this, the statistics always under-report what is actually happening. This is especially scary because the statistics are already high, and we are seeing an increase in data breaches of large companies and government organizations. Furthermore, the statistics are drawn from the date the identity theft is reported, not when it occurred. If there is an epidemic of people stealing kids' social security numbers, we may not see the statistics of those attacks for five, ten, or more years: that is, not until the kids apply for credit.

In general, we have a false sense of security and privacy on the Internet. Many people use their own devices, on their own wifi connection and believe no one can see what they are doing. They feel as if no one knows what they are doing on the Internet. They feel safe from being hacked or having their identity stolen, even though they probably know someone who's been a victim. In reality, to hackers, the Internet is a giant parking lot full of cars with expensive stuff in them, with all the doors unlocked and no security or gates preventing them from stealing everything they can grab. Sure, there are a few security guards in the parking lot chasing criminals. But there is only one guard for every 10,000 cars, and too many lurking criminals to chase them all.

If it is so easy and everyone is so vulnerable, then why haven't you been attacked already? First, there are many companies and institutions working hard on your behalf to keep the information you have with them safe. Second, it's less a matter of if you will be the victim of some form of identity or credit card theft, and more a matter of when and how it affects you. Since criminals will often take the path with the least risk and highest reward, they will prey on the easiest targets first. I think of this much like how lions hunt gazelles at the outside of the pack; the thing keeping them safe is the sheer number of other gazelles in the herd. More often than not, you are not the gazelle on the outside; eventually, you will find that you are. By reading this book and implementing what you've learned, you will significantly reduce your chances of being hit by identity theft and fraud, and when you are hit, you will significantly reduce the impact — turning what could be a life-changing ordeal into a minor inconvenience.

Did you know?

▶ Cyber crime is a $3.8 billion industry, larger than the global black markets in marijuana, cocaine, and heroin combined[4]
▶ In 2013, ~ 2.9 million identity theft incidents were reported[5]

Convenience vs. Security and Privacy

When using technology, we are constantly faced with the decision of trading off security for convenience. Today most people choose convenience every chance they get, but often they don't realize how much security they are sacrificing with that decision.

Every person has an understandably different level of security needs. You will need to make a decision about what level of security and convenience is right for you. A major principle of this book is to help you realize that you are opting for convenience on things you absolutely should not be. You will also learn that a minor compromise of convenience can lead to substantially better security.

You should also take into account that whatever length of time you are saving by choosing convenience over security now, is in most cases not even close to the amount of time it would take to recover from an attack. It can take exponentially longer to fix your credit report after identity theft than to simply prevent it from happening.

Remember

Being prepared before disaster strikes will save time and give you peace of mind.

You will also find that in the digital age, there are frequent opportunities to make trade-offs between convenience and privacy. And even more importantly, there are times when a lack of privacy (or inability to protect your privacy) can significantly increase your security vulnerabilities. The fact is, security is never absolute. My mother always said, "If they really want to break into your car, they will." I believe this saying applies directly to our identities online. We do simple things to protect our vehicles from break-ins, like parking them in well-lit, populated areas, rolling up the windows, locking the doors, and not leaving valuables in the car. You might even get a car alarm or a low-jack system installed. Taking these precautions increases the level of risk of getting caught for a car thief, and such deterrents will generally convince most common criminals to move along to an easier target. However, if you have a very specific car that certain criminals are targeting, and the criminals are not your average smash-and-grab opportunists, they will simply pick up your car with a tow truck and drive off. Security can be a cat-and-mouse game, especially if you and your possessions are being specifically targeted.

There are several different kinds of attacks that you could be subject to, including:

1. Large-scale attacks on organizations or communities that have your data, such as websites you use, healthcare facilities, educational institutions, and the like

2. Large-scale attacks targeted directly at consumers, such as credit-card skimmers, computer viruses, and phishing emails

3. Targeted attacks in which you have been specifically selected and pursued

Throughout this book, we will discuss several ways to help protect yourself from all three of these.

Inside each type of attack, there is a primary angle for the hacker's method of acting against you. Some may look to take over or use an existing account you have. Others may attempt to open a new line of credit or new account under your identity. Some may try to refinance your home, file taxes under your name, or use your name when being arrested or committing a crime. There is also affinity fraud, which are investment scams targeted towards specific groups of people – for example, Bernard Madoff's defrauding of organizations like Yeshiva University (and many individual investors) via his pyramid scheme. If all of this isn't bad enough, there are plenty more targeting you, your family, and yes, even your children.

How I stole my friend's identity

I'd like to share a story with you, as it demonstrates many of the things you will learn in this book. I was having a few drinks with my friend Michael when we stumbled into a conversation about identity theft. I mentioned how relatively easy it is to completely steal someone's identity.

Michael said, "Do you think you could steal my identity if you tried?"

"Absolutely," I replied.

After saying "Hmm…," pausing for a moment, and looking at me with a casual look of disbelief, he said, "Do it — I'm curious to see what you can come up with."

He felt as if he was fairly safe and secure and somewhat savvy about what to look out for.

I waited a couple of weeks so his guard would be down. Then I started out as if I only knew three things:

his first name, his last name, and what he looked like. Any other information or connection I had to him was not leveraged to my advantage. The first thing I did was find his Facebook account by using Google. I found he had enabled most of the privacy settings so people who weren't his friends couldn't see his data. To get this data, I'd need to send Michael a friend request from a fake account. He'd expect that you might say. Well, I was able to see a few of Michael's friends listed on his private profile. I simply picked one of his current friends pictures and used their picture and name on my new fake profile. I sent the invite his way and waited. Because the name and picture looked familiar, he accepted!

By getting to see his "private" Facebook profile, I was able to collect the following information:

- ► The name of his relatives and their relationship (he had them all tagged)
- ► The elementary and high school he attended
- ► Phone number
- ► City he was from (probably same as born in)
- ► Email

Not bad for an hour's worth of work. I was also able to find his dog's name by looking at the comments on his pictures.

Next, I checked to see if he had a LinkedIn profile—sure enough, he did. I was able to see every place he had previously worked and what college he attended—this could come in handy too.

Then I used some of the common people searching tools available on the Internet. I put in Michael's name and his city, which I got from LinkedIn and Facebook. Sure enough, there was a match from some public records from when he bought his house. Now I have his home address, and using Google maps I could see a picture from above and street view. A bit creepy, right? There was also a white Toyota Tacoma parked in his driveway on the street view picture: noted.

I also did more searches through public data sites and was able to get his parents' and his grandparents' names, including maiden names.

At this point, I'm really only missing one piece of crucial information—his social security number. For people born before 2011, the first five digits were assigned based on state and location, as well as the year. I know his birthday, and I know where he was probably born from his Facebook information. Cross-referencing that with publicly available data of everyone's social security number who has died, I was able to narrow down the first 5 of his social security number to seven options. What about the last four digits, you say? This is the fun part.

I asked a female friend of mine, Mary, to help out with this. Earlier when I was creeping through Michael's previous posts on Facebook, I noticed he mentioned an issue with his Comcast TV service. So I coached Mary on how to do a little social engineering and we gave Michael a call and made the caller ID appear as 1-800-COMCAST (we'll cover how to pull off such an awesome trick later in the book). Here is how the call went:

Michael: Hello?

Mary: Hi, may I speak with Michael Smith.

Michael: I'm Michael.

Mary: Hi Michael, my name is Rose and I'm calling from Comcast as part of our customer loyalty program. We know many people in your area have been having issues with their service over the past few weeks, so we wanted to apologize for that and apply a discount to your account for the inconvenience and to say thank you for your loyalty as a customer. We'd like to offer you a $25 credit to your bill.

Michael: Okay, awesome!

Mary: Great, well let me pull up your account so I can credit your bill. Michael, I'm just going to need to validate your identity. Your address is "321 Park Street," correct?

Michael: Yes.

Mary: What is your zip code?

Michael: 90210.

Mary: Perfect, and finally the last four of your social?

Michael: 9131.

Mary: Great! Well Michael, I have applied that $25 discount to your account, and you will see it applied to this month's bill when you get it.

Michael: Great!

Mary: Thank you so much again for being a loyal customer, we really appreciate your business.

Michael: Thank you, have a good one.

Mary: You too, bye now!

Surprisingly easily right? We'd all like to think we wouldn't fall for such a thing, but the truth of the matter is most people will and do. In this book, I will teach you to protect yourself from situations exactly like this.

So with the last four digits of his social security number, I signed him up for a credit monitoring service and tried each of the first seven social digits I had predicted before in combination with the last four. On attempt #3, I found the lucky winner. At this point I knew everything I needed to know about Michael to completely steal his identity, open a bank account, a credit card, and more. But I decided to take it a little further.

Knowing his email, I went to his email provider and did a forgot password request. It asked for the first name of his oldest niece/nephew and his elementary school. Remember how I could see his family members on Facebook because he tagged them? You guessed it. I was able to reset the password on his email account, which I promptly handed back over to him. However, with full control of someone's email account, you can easily see what banks they get emails from, if they have a PayPal or Amazon account, and what websites or services they frequent. With control of their email and the knowledge of all their "personal" information, an attacker could easily do password resets on most websites. Some websites may send the victim a text message upon resetting the account password, but if I were to deploy such an attack maliciously, I'd wait until he was on vacation or going to be without cell phone reception for an extended period. And of course, it'd be easy to know he was leaving for vacation when he tags himself at the airport with a comment bragging about how he is heading to a tropical island. There really isn't anything preventing me at this point from opening a credit card under his name. I can then use that credit card to pay movers and use my lock pick set to get in his house before they arrive. Think about it, if you have used movers: did they actually do anything at all to validate that you owned the stuff or residence you are paying them to move?

Truth is weirder than fiction: this has actually happened. In Wichita, Kansas, a man walked into the local police station and told them he was an undercover agent who had assumed the identity of a local man as he worked on a case. He wanted them to be up to speed: if anyone accused him of being an imposter, he said, they should reassure the accuser that everything was legit. Unfortunately (for him), the man was not a smooth talker, and the police began a routine investigation to check up on his identity. As it turned out, when the local man went for an extended stay with his ailing mother, the "secret agent" assumed his identity, got a fistful of new credit cards, and moved into his home, even securing a second mortgage for it. His only fumble was trying to explain himself at the police station.[6]

Now, I didn't steal any of Michael's stuff. I sat down to dinner with him and showed him all I had come up with. Needless to say, he was shocked. Like most people, he felt significantly safer than he should have. The look on his face when I played a tape of the fake Comcast call was priceless. He immediately recognized the mistake he had made.

Online, our identifying information isn't neatly tucked in a drawer or wallet. In this chapter, we've seen that all kinds of information and assets – from a pet's name to a social security number – are vulnerable. It takes more simple determination than master coding skills to get hold of an individual's most sensitive identifying information.

So how can we learn to see potential missteps and red flags, and then keep a healthy distance from them? The answer isn't exciting: it starts with habit. In the next chapter, we'll turn to the essential building blocks of a secure online identity: usernames, passwords, and authentication.

ONE

Authentication & Account Management

Importance of strong passwords

ONSUMERS SECURE almost everything with passwords. From email to bank accounts, from every website you have an account with, to your phone, your computer, and so on — your passwords are an important cornerstone and play a significant role in how we use technology. And yet most people have never received formal training on passwords. For example, are you using the same password for every website? Are you constantly forgetting your passwords and logins? What is a good password? A bad password? What are the best practices for having a good password? What happens if your password is hacked or stolen? Are your security questions easily discoverable, the way Michael's were?

Even if you believe you have your passwords under control, I recommend reading this chapter carefully. If you are thinking of skimming by because you are already pretty savvy and use a password manager application, you may be surprised by how much you can still learn. Even if you implement a better security practice by using unique random passwords on every website and storing them in a password manager, you are trading convenience for security. Although you've invested in a tool where all your passwords are protected by one master password, you are at risk of that password being discovered and used against you.

For example, in 2014, hundreds of private and nude photos, including some belonging to celebrities Jennifer Lawrence and Kate Upton, were posted on free message boards by hackers who were able to discover their victims' passwords. Apple reported at the time, "After more than 40 hours of investigation, we have discovered that certain celebrity accounts were compromised by a very targeted attack on user names, passwords and security questions, a practice that has become all too common on the Internet."[7] Many of the passwords were discovered via the simple, "brute-force" method of trial and error. This is something to keep in mind next time you are prompted to use a new password: should you create (and memorize) a new one, or use the predictable one you know you'll remember? Each precaution comes with its particular trade-off.

Did you know?

▶ 21% of people use passwords that are over 10 years old, and 54% of people use 5 or fewer passwords across their entire online life[8]

Remembering unique passwords

You have accounts on dozens of websites: how are you supposed to remember a unique password for all of them? You might wonder, "Why do I even need to do that?"

Tip

It is important to use unique passwords for every website, so that if hackers get hold of your password on one website, they don't have the keys to the entire kingdom.

By having unique passwords on each website, you are limiting what they can do with any password they obtain to one website—simple enough, right? I'd like to show you some ways to have unique passwords—or more variability at a minimum— without having to memorize a daunting stack of information.

 **Remember**

Do not store your passwords in a spreadsheet on your computer. If you have trouble remembering your username and passwords, follow the suggestions in the following section.

First, let's talk about what a good password is. A good password:

- ► has 10 characters or longer (but let's shoot for 12+)

- ► does not contain a noun (person, place, or thing), name, or any word

- ► does not contain keyboard sequences (asdf, qwerty, or 123456)

- ► must contain:

- ► upper case letters (ABCD)

- ► lower case letters (abcd)

- ► numbers (1234567890)

- ► special characters (~!@#$%^&*()_+<>?)

Now that we understand the rules our ideal passwords should follow, let's move on to the next step. Stop thinking of a password as simply a set of characters you need to memorize. Instead, let's come up with a system.

Base Password

Start with a base password—this will be your building block or the meat of the password. As mentioned above, this should not be a word or name of any kind: pick a few random characters on the keyboard.

Tip

Personally, I spend a few minutes experimenting to ensure these are characters I can type smoothly and consistently. I also take into account how hard it would be for someone to see by simply watching over my shoulder. If you poke at the keyboard with two fingers (or the 3-finger claw), then this may not apply to you—anyone watching will easily be able to see your password being typed. People who use default hand positions and type proficiently with all fingers will have an advantage at making their password harder to see as it is being typed.

Let's say you picked the characters:

```
1Kdc9)sfJ
```

I spent less than two minutes coming up with this base password, but take a look at my thought process. You might want to go to a keyboard and try to type this while you read it to understand it better:

- ▶ I started with 1kdc because I can type it quickly and consistently.

- ▶ Then, by using two characters on my left hand, I'm able to move my right-hand middle and ring finger to the nine and zero position.

- ▶ While pressing the zero, I simply engage the shift key with my left pinky to get the right parentheses.

- ▶ Then I allow my left hand to type two more characters while allowing my right hand to reset to the default position and press j.

- ▶ Then I revised the password to make the K and J upper-case. Since my left pinky never leaves the shift key, this works quite well.

- ▶ Because I can type it quickly and you never really know when the shift key is on or off, you'd probably have to video record it to figure out what I typed.

I don't expect you to have the exact same thought process, but I do want to stress the point that you should take some time to think about why you are making your password what it is. Since this is all random, you would need to commit to memorizing this base password—just do it! If this is something you are feeling overwhelmed about, the Acronym Method explained later in this chapter might be a better option for you.

Did you know?

▶ Surveys from 2014 show the most popular passwords were based on the following words:
```
123456
password
qwerty
baseball
iloveyou
football⁹
```

Capitalization and Number Location

Based on the Trustwave Global Security Report 2015 and analysis they did on a large dataset of passwords, "Business users are most likely to choose an uppercase letter (U) at the beginning of a password, fill the middle with lowercase letters (L) and append numbers (N) at the end."[10]

CHARACTER TYPE & SEQUENCE	PERCENTAGE
ULLLLLNN	4.97%
ULLLLLLN	4.41%
ULLLLLLNN	3.42%
ULLLLLLLN	3.16%
ULLLNNNN	2.67%
ULLLLNNN	2.45%
ULLLLLNNNN	2.44%

CHARACTER TYPE & SEQUENCE	PERCENTAGE
ULLLLLLLNN	2.41%
ULLLLNNNN	2.15%
ULLLLLLLNNNN	1.66%

This means if you are only capitalizing the first character of your password and placing numbers at the end, then your password fits the format for the most common 30% of passwords. These are the patterns that an attacker is going to try first.

Acronym Method

You can create an acronym from a longer phrase to use as your password. For example: "I wish John's birthday were December 1, 1990!" which you could then turn into "Iw-JbwD1,90!" This meets the minimum requirements for a password, including both lower and upper case letters, numbers, and two symbols, and length. Also, note that I didn't use the year of John's actual birthday, but rather what I wished—using the actual year of any major event of your life is a bad idea. This includes anniversaries, birth dates, graduations, etc.

Another example would be: "Our family loves to play chess every two years at the family reunion." You could turn that into: "Ofltpce2y@tfr."

The problem with using the acronym method is that you end up with the same password on every website. However, you can use a shorter acronym and treat it as your base password, and then use the following techniques to make your password unique at each website.

Variability

Time to add some variability. This is essential: while it's good that you have a strong base password, it needs to be different for every website you use. Here are some systems you can implement or use them as inspiration to come up with your own system.

Domain Method

Every website we go to has a domain name, facebook.com, bankofamerica.com, etc. For this next method, we'll use one or more parts of that domain to help make our passwords different between websites. First you should be able to identify the root part of the domain. The root domain is the part directly before the TLD (the .com, .net, or .org). Today there are many different types of TLD's .gov, .info, .ninja, .tips, .io, '.co.uk' and many more to identify. For help in identifying the TLD check out this write-up:

Resource: Identifying the root domain

`http://dsg.tips/domain`

You also have to ensure you aren't looking at a subdomain; this usually prefixes the root domain. For example, for api. facebook.com or mobile.bankofamerica.com, we only care about the root domains, "facebook" and "bankofamerica". For this method to work consistently, you have to use the root domain (and you could also use the TLD, but using the TLD is not recommended as it will reduce the variability.)

There are dozens of different methods you could use but for this example, I will use the last two characters of the root domain. I will also prefix this to my password. So, for example, when I log into facebook.com my full password would be:

```
oklKdc9)sfJ
```

In this example "ok" comes from the last two characters of the root domain, facebook.com, and the base password:

```
lKdc9)sfJ
```

Here is another example for bankofamerica.com:

```
calKdc9)sfJ
```

Wow, is that password looking significantly more complex than the one you are using now? In the end, your password should be nine characters you have to memorize (I believe in you!), with a prefix of the last two characters of the root domain. Sure, this might feel complicated compared to what you were doing before, but the system is simple at heart. With minimal effort, it will make your accounts significantly more secure.

Some other variations of this method could be the first and last letter of the root domain; the second letter of the root domain but capitalized, or the last letter of the root domain and the last letter of the TLD. I recommend using two letters as using one limits you to 26 different combinations; you will find a decent amount of overlap. Adding the second letter is easy and significantly increases variability.

Categories

Categories are a bit more advanced than the Domain Method, so you may not want to adopt this right away. However, when you are comfortable, combining this with the Domain Method can be really effective. Categorize the types of websites you are using and assign them a letter(s). For example:

▶ b = Banking, anything financial related or that you pay a bill to

▶ s = Social Media, Facebook, LinkedIn, Twitter, etc.

▶ e = Email

▶ o = Other

I recommend you keep the categories simple and limited in number until you feel more comfortable. Use a system that works for you and that you will remember. One simple twist would be to select the last character of each category (g for banking, a for social media, l for email, etc. or make them capital letters, or shifted one key to the left on the keyboard, v instead b, a instead of s, w instead of e). Once you have a category list and a designated set of characters, determine a location in your base password to place it. You could prefix it, insert it somewhere in the middle, or as in our example case, add it onto the end.

Using the original base password I came up with, "1Kdc9)sfJ", this is what it would look like when logging into Facebook:

`1Kdc9)sfJs`

Or email:

`1Kdc9)sfJe`

This, at least, segregates passwords for different parts of our life on the Internet. It is more likely that your password will be compromised on an untrusted or "other" website than it will be from a bank.

Gotchas & Misc.

Some websites will only allow specific special characters. This could potentially mess up your password memorization system. If your special character is on a number key, I recommend you replace it with the corresponding number. If it is not, I recommend having a replacement letter or number for each of the special characters you have in your password to deal with this scenario.

Most websites require a specific password length, which can pose a challenge in some cases. Your base password should ensure you meet this standard on 99% of websites, which means it should be 8-10 characters long at a minimum before adding the additional variability characters. You should never worry about your password being too long: the longer it is, the better it is.

Rarely, websites will redirect to a different root domain during login—you will just have to be conscious of this issue, and it is very rare. You will also have to modify your system for when creating passwords on mobile applications. To help ensure consistency with my system, I will use the website URL of the mobile application to create a password to use on that app.

Some websites you register on will probably seem less legitimate, possibly spam-ridden, or otherwise untrustworthy in some way. In these cases, I always use a junk password, by which I mean a random password that doesn't relate to my normal system. That way, if my account gets compromised or the password is leaked, it won't harm me in any way. Keep a lookout for this scenario and use a junk password when appropriate. I also use this if I am forced to register for something that is not on my computer—for example, on a shared computer at a conference booth or sign-up desk. You can always change it later.

Did you know?

▶ This table shows how long it would take a hacker to decipher your password, based on length (and assuming the password already includes upper and lower-case letters and numbers):[11]

Length (characters)	Time
8	~1 day
10	~5 years
12	~25,000 years

To test the strength of your new password, checkout this resource:

Resource:
How secure is your password

....

`http://dsg.tips/pass`

....

Social Logins

There has been a dramatic increase on the Internet of the ability to log into a website using one of your other accounts. This could be your Google, Facebook, LinkedIn, Twitter, etc. These systems have had their share of security concerns but are now generally considered safe. There are only two cautions I have when using these. First, if your Facebook account becomes compromised, the attacker could access any site you use with your Facebook account. Same goes for any other social network login. Second, you are often providing personal information such as your name and email, sometimes even the ability for them to see what you have posted and your likes and interests. If they are requesting access to it, they are probably collecting it. Keep an eye out for websites requesting access to information they definitely don't need and consider using an alternative sign-up method when this happens. At best, they want to use your information for marketing purposes, but there's always a chance they may have more nefarious purposes in mind.

Password management tools

Even with the new system you just learned, you might be having a hard time remembering all those logins. Maybe you prefer the convenience of one-click login or like having a list of all your accounts in one organized place. If that's the case, there are some options. In more recent years, several tools and methods have become available that make password management significantly easier. So, should you be using one of these tools? Are they safe?

From a convenience and organizational standpoint, these tools are awesome: they let you generate long random passwords for each website you use. If you don't have a need to log into sites when that tool isn't around, these strong random passwords are ideal. These programs are also significantly better than that insecure spreadsheet or text document you may be using to store passwords.

However, from a security standpoint, you have now just put every username and password you have into one central database. If you were a hacker, this is exactly the type of thing you'd target. Sure, your information is encrypted and protected by a master password that you set. However, if your computer became infected with a virus, it could capture the keys you press on your keyboard when unlocking your password database. Hackers could then decrypt or simply just extract all the passwords after you unlocked it.

Most security experts would not promote a database that has all your passwords in it that you unlock with one password, especially if you are typing and unlocking it frequently. However, if you do your due diligence on keeping your computer secure and virus/malware free, this is definitely better than simply using the same, easily guessed password on every website. Another benefit of password managers is they will alert you should a site on which you have an account has been hacked.

I do think having a secure list of all the websites on which you have accounts is a good idea. It can be really useful to know precisely where your accounts are, from the obvious (email) to the more incidental (that yoga studio where you took a free class once). That list of websites will come in handy when you need to update all your passwords.

This is one of those occasions when you need to weigh the importance of convenience vs. security. The convenience and benefits of these password management tools make them an attractive option. The best level of security, though, would not be using one of these. And don't even think of using a password manager if your computer could be infected with a virus or malware. For example, I wouldn't use it on a computer that a 14-year-old uses—they tend to wander the Internet and open things they shouldn't. They lack the "Internet safety common sense" that we have all come to know.

All that being said, if the password manager route is the one that works best for your needs, here are a couple tools I would recommend using.

Resource: Password managers

http://dsg.tips/password

You'll find that some browsers have a built-in feature to help you remember your password. These have been subject to security issues in the past but have made significant progress. As of this writing, I recommend disabling your browser's "remember password" feature and use a proper password manager like those recommended above.

Many of these password managers will also include the ability to store addresses, credit card numbers, and other important document details. I advise against this, as you are really putting all your valuables in one basket: if the whole basket is hacked or stolen, you will regret it.

If you are using a password manager and want to have an increased level of security, consider leaving a character or two off of your passwords. More specifically, I recommend you use the Domain Method described earlier. This way, even if your entire password database were stolen unencrypted, none of the passwords would work because they are missing one or more characters. This would add the task of having to type two letters into the memorized password every time you want to access an online account, but it's a good way to balance convenience and security.

Rotating passwords

You may have heard before that you should rotate your passwords regularly, but why? Your password could be stolen, for example, but that data could lie dormant after a major hack while hackers wait for the investigation to cool off. Months or even years later, that data could be sold on the black market; your trusty old password could become a commodity itself.

How often should you be changing your passwords? Most corporations will never allow you to keep a password for more than 90 days, and they will restrict your ability to reuse an old password. Since the password you use at work should be different than the passwords you use for your personal life, you should come up with a method that works for you so that you can rotate your passwords and not forget them. For your personal passwords, changing the password on dozens of accounts every 90 days is clearly very cumbersome. I recommend you change them yearly at a minimum. When doing your yearly password updates, don't even think about simply adding the last two digits of the year to your base password: that is one of the first variations a hacker would try. By the same token, change more than just a couple letters—taking a shortcut is only trading off short-term convenience against security.

Did you know?

► Your legal rights regarding data and passwords start with the following:

► Police cannot search the data on your computer, laptop or cell phone without a warrant unless you give them consent.

► Police can search your electric devices at a border crossing without a warrant.

► You do not have to provide your password to police, even if they have a warrant to search your device. It is considered self-incriminating testimony and covered under the Fifth Amendment.

► You can only be forced, under rare special circumstances, to provide your password by a judge or grand jury.

Choosing a username

Usernames are also identifiers that we should spend a little bit of time thinking about. When joining a website, you may be asked to choose a username. Generally speaking, most websites should simply use your email as your username, unless that website will be sharing your username with other users— on a forum or marketplace, for example. With that in mind, your username can reveal a lot about you, especially if you put your full name in it and end it with the last two digits of the year you were born. If it isn't publicly displayed, this may not be a big deal, but if it is, you may want to be more conscious about selecting your username.

Your username can also be used to link public activity across the Internet. By simply Googling your username, someone may be able to see what you have been up to on the Internet. This may not be an issue unless you start to mix business and personal activities. For example, you may be a doctor who likes to provide free advice on forums both professionally and for fun. But you don't want to also use that same username where you talk about controversial or personal issues that you may not want associated with your professional opinion or career.

From a security standpoint, it would probably be best to use a unique username for each website that contains no information about or related to you. For most people, the inconvenience of this method makes it unrealistic. If you'd rather opt to remember just one username, I recommend that you select one that will not be common. Specifically, use 3 or 4 numbers at the end of the username. That will greatly reduce the odds that it already exists. If you choose the username bob, chances are it will be taken. If you choose bob08 or bob84, chances are it will be taken. Then you will have to deal with remembering a bunch of different usernames because some variations were taken on some websites. Chances are bob135 will be available. I also recommend you choose a base username that does not contain anything about you or related to you. Don't use your favorite pet's name and then use that same pet in your forgot password question. Don't use your year of birth or graduation, as that will just leak more information about yourself. Don't use PIN numbers, passwords, social security numbers, or any other sort of personal information.

Keep in mind a unique username will be more convenient in the long run, as you won't run into the issue of it being taken already. However, it does allow an attacker targeting you to most likely guess your username to most websites with which you have an account. Additionally, if that website publishes your username publicly, like on a forum, it will be very easy for people to search for your username and uniquely identify things you have said or posted on the Internet. Try searching for some of the usernames you have used in the past to see what comes up on Google. This will give you an idea of what someone else can find out about you when they try to poke around, trying to discover what, if anything, they can about you.

Remember

You may want to set up two usernames for yourself: one professional, and one that allows you to post freely about controversial or personal issues.

If you need inspiration looking for a good username, I recommend you pick your favorite character from your favorite TV or movie. This might make it more popular and common to run into collisions where other people already have it, but your numbers or spelling tweaks will help reduce that significantly.

When picking an email handle, you should follow the same guidelines and advice. A professional email address will probably be your full name, but it should not include your birth year.

Two-factor authentication

Two-factor authentication can add a significantly higher level of security to your identity. So what is it? Basically, you can think of logging in with a password as single-factor authentication. If someone gets your password, they can get in using that one factor. With two-factor, there is generally a password that you know, and then a second code you have to enter at the same time to access the account. This code could be sent to your phone via a text message or phone call. In this scenario, your identity is validated by ensuring not only that the password is correct, but that you currently have access to the phone number on the account. When you are protected like this, even if someone gets your password, they won't be able to get the code from your phone when they try to log in unless they also steal your phone. At first this may seem like significantly more effort when logging into your account. And indeed, it can be in some situations. Some websites are configurable so that you only have to use two-factor if you are accessing it from a new location or device. This gives you the best mix of security and convenience, as you won't have to enter it as often.

In addition to the code being sent to your phone, there are also apps like Google Authenticator and Authy that contain a six-digit code that changes every 30 to 60 seconds. The code rotates in a way that the website you are visiting then knows what the six digit code should be at any given time.

A 2012 Wired article detailed the experience of technology journalist Mat Honan, who—because he failed to use two-factor authentication—had his entire digital life destroyed by one very savvy hacker in the span of just one hour. One by one, his accounts toppled: first his Google account was taken over, then deleted; next his Twitter was compromised, blasting racist, homophobic messages, to his horror; finally, his Apple iCloud account was broken into, and before he could blink an eye, every last bit of data on his iPhone, iPad, and MacBook was deleted.

Though it may sound harsh to say, this was partially Mat's fault. Why? His accounts shared enough login information that they were effectively daisy-chained together: once the hacker accessed his Amazon account, he had enough information to access his Apple ID account, email, and finally Twitter. Had he enabled two-factor authentication for his Google and iCloud accounts, this unfortunate turn of events very likely would have been avoided. Mat lost a year's worth of work, photos of his young daughter, and emails and documents that he hadn't stored anywhere else. (As it turned out, the hacker was after something laughably mundane: he liked Mat's three-character-long Twitter handle.) How many times have you thought to yourself, "I should be backing this up somewhere, but I'll get to it?" That question alone is a very good reason to use two-factor authentication.[12]

You might be wondering, when evaluating your security needs for different types of websites, which ones necessitate two-factor authentication? Email is definitely the number one candidate. If you aren't using two-factor authentication to protect your email, then fix that immediately: it is a free option for most email services. Because email contains so much information about yourself, and can usually be used to reset the password to any other account you have, it is the primary target for hackers. They can also use it to more reliably spread viruses, as people are more likely to open an email from you than some random email address. After your email, you should enable it for anything having to do with your financials. Many banks and financial institutions are now making this a requirement, and you may have been using two-factor authentication without even realizing it. I also highly recommend you enable two-factor authentication for any cloud, sync, or backup you may use, especially iCloud. Finally, if you are in the media or have any significant following on your social media sites, you should also enable two-factor authentication on your social media sites as well.

For an in-depth tutorial of how to set up two-factor authentication on popular websites and get the right apps on your phone, check out this link:

Resource:
Two-factor authentication guide

`http://dsg.tips/twofactor`

The next frontier in two-factor authentication is likely to be biometrics. Fingerprint usage and validation, for instance, are becoming increasingly popular.

Remember

Use two-factor on your email, financial accounts, any cloud sync/backup accounts, and healthcare accounts. If a service you use does not already support two-factor authentication, you should contact their support and request support for it.

Always log out

From time to time, you may have to log into a website on a computer that is not yours. Usually when you are finished with a website, you would simply close the tab or browser and move on. When using a computer that is not yours, especially if it is a public computer, you need to be sure to manually log out of the website. You should also do this anytime you use public, insecure, or shared wifi networks.

I also recommend you manually log out of high-risk websites like financial institutions, even if you are using your own computer. If a hacker were to highjack your session (steal the cookie from your computer), then they may be able to use the website as if they were logged in as you. In this scenario, when you manually select logout, it would actually force them out. By doing this, you would limit your exposure, and although this won't save most people, it isn't that much effort to create a good habit.

For other sites like social networks, you often visit these frequently and logging in and out may be too inconvenient for you. That is a trade-off you need to be comfortable with, but you must log out of social network sites if you use a public or insecure wifi or public computer.

Why the public wifi? Well, Facebook now forces all users to use SSL at all times. You may know SSL as HTTPS or as a secure connection. It is important to note that when using HTTPS, you are using an encrypted connection, not necessarily a secure one. There once was a time when you could go on Facebook via HTTP, aka an unencrypted connection. This allowed someone on the same wifi network to steal your cookie and highjack your session, i.e., start surfing Facebook as if they were logged in as you. Some savvy developers then created a tool to make this entire process point and click, so even the most novice computer users could go to a Starbucks and start taking over other people's accounts. Although today Facebook requires you to be on an encrypted connection, you should always confirm you are using SSL/HTTPS/secure browsing when submitting any information. Many websites don't force you to use a secure connection unless you are logging in or entering payment information. However, moving forward you will see more websites forcing SSL for all page, which is a good thing.

Final thoughts

You may also find that websites you have accounts with are at some point hacked. When this happens, it is recommended that you immediately change your password. Obviously, this is going to mess with your fancy new password management strategy. This will likely happen to you eventually, so it is best to prepare for how you will handle it. You could change a few characters so you are not the easy target. Alternatively, you could try using your next password—the password you will use when you change it next year. Also, pay attention to if your forgot password questions and answers were leaked in the attack. If they were, your other accounts might be at an increased risk even if they were using a different password.

Simple methods and tricks that come to mind have also come to the minds of many before you. There is evidence of this from data analysis of passwords that were leaked from large-scale hacks on public websites. There is also evidence of this from analysis of leaked PIN numbers. For example, the PIN number 2580 showed up as an anomaly. Turns out 2580 is the sequence straight down the middle of the keypad. Although these ideas are sometimes effective at first, after thousands and tens of thousands of people begin to use the same technique, it becomes a statistical anomaly that hackers prey on.

Did you know?

▶ An analysis of 3.4 million PIN numbers found that 26.83% passwords were one out of 20 most commonly used passwords, as below: [13]

Rank	PIN	Freq.
#1	1234	10.713%
#2	1111	6.016%
#3	0000	1.881%
#4	1212	1.197%
#5	7777	0.745%
#6	1004	0.616%
#7	2000	0.613%
#8	4444	0.526%
#9	2222	0.516%
#10	6969	0.512%
#11	9999	0.451%
#12	3333	0.419%
#13	5555	0.395%
#14	6666	0.391%
#15	1122	0.366%
#16	1313	0.304%
#17	8888	0.303%
#18	4321	0.293%
#18	2001	0.290%
#19	1010	0.285%

Finally, make sure your backup or forgot password options are set up and up to date. These can include your phone number or a secondary email address on your accounts. Even if you aren't hacked, these are your lifelines if you forget your account information.

There are some services that will monitor your information on the Internet and some that even collect data from large hacks. You can see if your information exists in the hacked data or place alerts to watch for your information showing up in the future. Although this won't alert you about all the data on the black market, it can notify you about the hacks where the data is released publicly. See them here:

Resource:
Monitor compromised information

http://dsg.tips/alert

Don't write down your password. This happens significantly more than it should, especially in the workplace. Writing down passwords may also legally expose you. Courts have ruled that you must produce a physical key to a secure device, but you do not have to provide a safe's code under the 5th amendment. Courts have ruled that passwords are more like safe combinations than strongbox keys, but writing down your password could potentially tilt that legal safety you have.[14] [15]

Interestingly, the rise in fingerprint-based authentication, mainly on the iPhone, actually provides you less protection from self-incrimination. A fingerprint is not considered testimony and like DNA is not protected by the 5th amendment. Essentially, if you use fingerprint authentication on your phone, the government can force you to unlock your phone (with a warrant), but if you only have a keyed password, which is only in your mind/memory, they cannot. Keep this in mind if you have a computer that supports fingerprint unlocking.

In this chapter, we've gone over usernames and passwords, and what choices can make them secure or vulnerable. In the next, we'll expand that approach to the area of our digital lives where we tend to share the most: social networks.

TWO

SOCIAL NETWORKS

MODERN SOCIAL networking websites that have attained mass adoption are a relatively new thing; most started in the last 10 to 15 years. This new technology has brought a new and heightened level of security risk that many people are unaware of.

Remember

Assume that anything you put on the Internet will be there forever and viewable by anyone. Even if you are posting it to a private audience of your close friends on a social network, assume everyone can view it, forever. It may change how and what you share online. You never know how that information will become available to a larger audience, but it could and will be impossible to truly erase.

For example, to go on a journey back in time, check out the Wayback Machine, a tool that has been archiving snapshots of websites on the Internet for nearly 20 years. You can see the first version of yahoo.com from 1996, cnn.com back in 2000, youtube.com in 2005, or any other website you can think of.

Resource: Wayback Machine

http://dsg.tips/wayback

Have you ever seen people post a privacy notice on their social network? Unfortunately, though well-intentioned, posting your own privacy notices will not protect you in any way. Some people also post privacy or confidentiality notices in the footer of their email. This is similarly useless, especially when communicating with people in other countries. In most cases it can't hurt you, but it also won't do anything to protect you.

According to the American Bar Association, "There is no legal doctrine or theory under which an email confidentiality disclaimer is enforceable in a circumstance like this. There is virtually no scholarly analysis of the impact of email disclaimers and very little analysis by non-scholars."[16]

There may be some cases in which it is beneficial for a lawyer or tax person to have one of these disclaimers, for example specifying when there is no client-attorney privilege or formal tax advice. These are the rare disclaimers that will be considered valid in a court of law.

Professional vs. personal identity

In this new age where sharing is so easy, people often blur the line between their personal and professional identities. It's important to establish a separate professional and personal identity on the Internet.

Tip

The professional identity should have public information and be easier for people to access—it is information you want people to see, even if you don't know them. Your personal profiles online should be more private and secure. You should limit who can view what you share, even in this network.

A good example of this is using LinkedIn for your professional information and Facebook for your personal information. In some cases, you may want a professional presence on Facebook as well. If this applies to you, I recommend that you create two separate accounts and separate your professional from your personal profile. Your Facebook will need to have very defined, locked-down privacy permissions. In reality, you don't even want your friends of friends to be able to see anything that you say or share, or any of your profile details. It may not sound like a big deal, but some of your friends have hundreds if not thousands of other friends, which means you're opening your information up to thousands to tens of thousands of people to see. There is really no benefit for people outside your immediate friends to have or see anything that you do on your personal social network account. If someone is trying to do a highly targeted attack against you and your permissions are open enough to let friends of friends see your information, it is probably quite easy for them to get one of your friends to accept them—they may not be as diligent about protecting themselves as you are. Setting your profile to "private" is not enough. You need to truly understand the permissions that apply to all the content and information you post.

For a detailed breakdown of recommended settings for popular social networks like Facebook, please check out this guide:

Resource:
Social network privacy settings

`http://dsg.tips/social`

Ensuring you know them

My advice is simple: do not add people that you do not know to your personal networks. I also recommend you be vigilant about who you add to your professional networks, especially if you're revealing personal information to people that you do know or have added as a friend.

On your personal network, you should never add someone that you don't know in real life, period. You may be encouraged to add them because there might be small indicators that you might know them. For example "this person is also friends with 14 of your other friends." Sure, this might be safer than a request from someone who isn't friends with any of your buddies, but it is also a false illusion of safety. If I made a fake profile and added all your friends, how many of them do you think are diligent enough to not add my fake profile? That person with 1,500 friends likely accepts most friend requests. Also, keep in mind if it makes sense that they are adding you. If you thought you were already friends with them and now you're getting an invite from them, before you impulsively click "accept," look at your friends list and see if they are still connected. If they are, then you should be very suspicious that someone may be using their name and photo to gain your trust and on-line "friendship," thus giving them access to more information about you. Profile pictures are publicly available on the social network, even with a private profile, and so are names—any novice computer user can leverage that to make a fake profile.

Don't act impulsively. People who are trying to exploit, scam, or take advantage of you are preying on the fact that most people will act impulsively or out of emotion. Online, we tend to lose our inhibitions. Take a moment to reflect on if the request makes sense. If you were out with friends last night and met someone new and the next day they sent you an invite, this scenario would make significantly more sense than an anonymous invite from an unfamiliar person pretending to know you from ten years ago.

Did you know?

- Facebook had ~1.44 billion monthly active users globally as of March 31, 2015. That is greater than the population of China (where Facebook is currently blocked).[17]
- Twitter had ~302 million monthly active users globally as of March 31, 2015. That's almost equivalent to the population of the United States.[18]
- LinkedIn has ~364 million registered members globally, greater than the population of the United States.[19]

Keep in mind that it is not just criminals who may be trying to look at your profile. Employers, police, insurance companies, financial underwriters, reporters, and others may also be attempting to take a peek into your life and history. There are even companies out there that are now using analysis of your social behavior online to score your likelihood of defaulting on a loan—think credit report based on public and social network activity you put out there on the Internet. Some life insurance companies have been known to analyze your public social data to identify your health and risk markers. So those pictures of you smoking a cigar while drinking Scotch? The endless shots of the late-night pizzas you enjoy a little too often? How about your daredevil streak that lures you into skydiving, base jumping, and swimming with sharks? The photos may get you tons of likes, but they are also great ways to have your insurance company classify you as higher risk. Keep them out of public view and keep your data private.

Be Careful what you share

The sheer amount of things that people post pictures of online is shocking—I'm not talking about those food pics but rather things like credit cards. You might think, well I'm not that stupid, but some people have just never been made aware of the consequences, or they think hiding some of the numbers protects them. Maybe you trust your friends wouldn't steal it, but you didn't realize your friends of friends can also see it. You actually might have posted things online that you didn't realize was possibly a bad idea. Some things that seem innocent can get you into a whole lot of trouble, fast.

This over-sharing happens much more than you think. Granted, it is usually younger people who don't know any better—but not always. When posting a credit card, people believe they're clever by covering the first set of numbers. What they don't realize is that the first few numbers are actually the same depending on what bank or credit institution they were issued from. Most American Express cards start with the same numbers, and Bank of America cards start with the same numbers, etc. By simply Googling which card you have, I can easily find out those first few numbers. Even hiding some numbers in the middle or near the end is fruitless—credit cards use a checksum digit as the last number. This means you can apply a math formula to all the numbers on your credit card, and the result will be the last digit of your credit card. Using this method, a hacker can use trial and error to brute-force guess the numbers you covered on your card. Bottom line, don't post it under any circumstance, even to a small group of friends.

Sharing this type of information was happening so often on sites such as Tumblr that hackers are now searching public picture posts every few seconds, looking for credit cards and then using OCR (optical character recognition) to automatically read that credit card number. The moment a credit card is posted online to the moment a transaction is charged on that credit card can be a mere matter of minutes.

There are many other things besides credit cards you shouldn't post: checks of any kind, gift cards of any kind, documents with your account number or social security number on them, your boarding pass, and definitely not your winning ticket at the horse races. This exact theft happened in fall 2015 to an Australian woman who gave her name only as Chantelle. Euphoric after watching the race, she posted a selfie with the winning betting slip on Facebook. She didn't realize the barcode could be deciphered and redeemed by anyone who wanted to claim the cash in her name. When she went to collect her winnings, she was told that a man had already swung by and swept them away.[20]

Proud of that brand new degree, so you post a picture of yourself holding it? Not only can I use that picture to make a fake degree, but I'm sure I can come up with some creative ways to manipulate my face instead of yours, or to change the degree you are holding in the image. People also post pictures of their security badges—again, thanks for providing me with a template! People are understandably proud of their big accomplishments, and they want to share with their friends and family, but they don't realize the harm that can come from sharing their joy too freely. Even if I don't use your security badge as a template, I can probably assume you posted that on your first day. I bet I could find an interesting way to use that piece of information to steal your identity or impersonate you.

An interesting one that many people don't think about is posting pictures of their keys online. It may not even be on purpose—perhaps you are taking a picture of the cute bear the barista made in the foam of your latte, but there your keys are in the background. Some computer scientists at UC San Diego demonstrated their ability to stand on a roof with a telephoto lens, take a picture of keys sitting on a table at a cafe about 200 feet away, then, using their software, they created an exact copy of the key — and this was back in 2008. [21]

More recently, the Washington Post unwittingly published an article about TSA baggage handling and included a picture of the master, luggage opening, keys the TSA uses. Lock-picking and security enthusiasts then used that picture to print homemade replica keys using their 3D printer. Now anyone can download the key design files and print their own TSA master keys on their home 3D printer. These days there are even apps you can download, to take a picture of your key and have a copy mailed to you. The concept is interesting: save a photo of your key, and if you ever lose it or get locked out, simply open the app and order a key, then pick it up at a local kiosk, an automated machine that will print you a copy. Other services can send you a key within a few days. Given a good picture, or a moment alone with someone's keys, you can create your own copy.

Dangers of Oversharing

Every time you tag a post of where you are, you could be providing criminals that information. I'm not into robbing houses, but if I were going to, I'd definitely be watching for your check-ins and vacation updates. My favorite is the vacation countdown and constant updates during that vacation. And just so I don't get caught red-handed, you do a countdown of your days remaining on vacation. Sometimes you do that heads-up notice that you are at the airport and headed back home. Don't think this could happen to you? Let's look at how it could happen.

- ▶ Criminal drives by your house and it catches their eye—maybe you had the garage open and some good stuff inside, or maybe a nice car.

- ▶ They search online for public records of who owns or lives at that address.

- ▶ They search your name on Google to find your Facebook.

- ▶ They take one of your visible friend's profiles, copy their name and photo to create a fake profile and then add you.

- ▶ You accept them thinking it is your friend; now they just watch and wait for you to tell them the safest time for them to break in.

The above was not something only sophisticated criminals can pull off—you might be thinking you could do that yourself and so could a 14-year-old kid. You also have to remember that if you are on vacation, you are probably not keeping a close eye on your financial accounts and email. When you go camping for a holiday weekend without cell phone reception, that is a perfect time for me to initiate a transfer from your bank account to mine. By the time you notice, the money will have already passed through the clearing house and will be harder to recover. Think twice about what you post, especially if you have weak privacy settings and a large number of friends in your network. I get that you're excited about your vacation, but consider waiting to share it until after you have returned home.

Don't post your phone number in posts or on your profile information—not even on your personal locked-down profile. If someone needs your number, they will send you a direct message. The same goes for your email.

Don't list your birthday and, more importantly, don't list your place of birth. If you absolutely must have your birthday publicly listed on Facebook, at least disable the year of birth from displaying. Honestly, though, change your birthday by a week and see how many of your friends wish you a happy birthday on Facebook. It will make for a good laugh!

Did you know?

▶ 90% of American adults think others divulge too much information online.[22]

If you have children, you probably love posting photos of them. You probably also put their name and you probably also posted their birthday. Your children's names and birthdays are ripe pieces of information for hackers looking to compromise your identity and maybe even steal it. If you have kids, make sure your social network is locked down.

And we've all seen those risqué or party photos online. Sometimes we wish we hadn't seen them. They probably seem like a great idea when the person is posting them, but not so great the next day. But no big deal, you can just delete them, right? Wrong. When considering if you should post a photo, it is safe to assume everyone can see it (even people you don't know or might know in the future) and that it can never be removed. Even if you delete it, it still exists online. Just ask yourself, is there any person I wouldn't want to share this with in the future?

People tend to use social networks as a confessional outlet, which can be an unfortunate misuse of the platform. Admitting to lying on your taxes, showing off large amounts of cash, drugs, or guns, how you pulled a quick one on an insurance agency—all bad ideas. You should follow the same rules as you do with photos. Even if your privacy settings are locked down, and you are diligent about whom you add, the police can still get a court order of all your Facebook posts and private chat conversations.

In this chapter, we've covered what it takes to use social networks privately, safely, and with dignity. You now know how to avoid being seen as a target. In the next chapter, we'll dive into the emotional manipulation that hackers prey on.

THREE

SOCIAL ENGINEERING

What is social engineering?

THE UNITED States Computer Emergency Readiness Team (US-CERT) defines social engineering as the following:

"In a social engineering attack, an attacker uses human interaction (social skills) to obtain or compromise information about an organization or its computer systems. An attacker may seem unassuming and respectable, possibly claiming to be a new employee, repairperson, or researcher and even offering credentials to support that identity. However, by asking questions, he or she may be able to piece together enough information to infiltrate an organization's network. If an attacker is not able to gather enough information from one source, he or she may contact another source within the same organization and rely on the information from the first source to add to his or her credibility."[23]

Social engineering can lead to a host of invasive crimes, ranging from large-scale corporate hacks to personal theft. "Social engineering is the biggest threat to the enterprise, without a doubt," says Shane MacDougall, who runs a security firm that focuses on corporate espionage. MacDougall knows what techniques to look for: he won a social engineering contest at the 2012 DEFCON, an annual underground hacking conference attended by hackers and security professionals alike. With a crowd watching, he secured confidential Wal-Mart records after a single call to a store manager in Arkansas, during which he persuaded the unsuspecting manager that he could win Wal-Mart a valuable government contract as long as he could provide some detailed information. Using a combination of advanced research and seamless on-the-spot acting, MacDougall gained all the information he was looking for in about 20 minutes. Talking to CNN, MacDougall concluded, "I see all these [chief security officers] that spend all this money on firewalls and stuff, and they spend zero dollars on awareness."[24]

Social Engineering is a common practice in hacking, happening every day at every level. Many people, when they hear the word "hacker" think of a nerdy guy clacking away on a home-built computer in a shadowy basement, gaining access to his ex's Facebook password. The truth is far more menacing. And spectacular. The truth? Hacking is big business.

Vice reporter Angela Hennessy recently sat down with a hacker named "Ghost" who specializes in offense security and social engineering. In a matter of minutes,

Ghost showed the Vice reporter some systems he had socially engineered his way into, including the technical back end of a major corporation whose earnings were in the tens of millions of dollars. Ghost was able to show Angela customers' full names, Social Security Numbers, direct deposit slips, home addresses, and phone numbers. Who knows, yours could have been one of them, such was the size and popularity of the company.

The truth is, no one is safe from people like Ghost. So how does he do it? Social Engineering.

Social Engineering relies on human interaction: Ghost summed up the social engineer's "toolkit" as communication (listening skills are imperative), patience, psychology, elicitation, intelligence gathering, deductive logic, and acting.[25]

The easiest way in is almost always the phone. Ghost picks the company he wants to target first. He knows he needs to get into the corporate office. He decides he's going to target one of the top executive assistants. She answers with first name only, "This is Amanda." He hangs up. He then goes to several websites and does research on Amanda—learns through her past email addresses, social media profiles, and Google history that she's a single mom, learns her favorite shows and music, and even accesses photos of her home. Finally, after about a month of research, he shows up at the company posing as a single dad coming for an interview. He shows up 30 minutes late and pretends to forget his resume. He immediately engages Amanda for help, knowing she will relate. He gives her a sob story about his babysitter and how he can't get a break and tells her how he really needs a job. Of course, Amanda sympathizes and agrees to print his resume, inserting his USB drive into her computer. The hitch? It has a virus, which will allow Ghost to remotely gain access to all the company's most sensitive information. And that's how he's in the café showing a Vice reporter thousands of consumers' personal information.

Although social engineering is commonly used to infiltrate companies and organizations, it is also used against consumers directly when criminals attempt to steal their money or identity. Having an understanding of what this looks like will help you to protect yourself from being a victim of this malicious practice in the future.

Cold calls

A cold call is when you receive a phone call that you were not expecting. When combined with social engineering, cold calls are an effective tool for hackers. These calls can seem and feel very legitimate. When the reality factor is high, and without raising any alarms in your head, this type of social engineering can easily lead you down a path of unwittingly compromising your information. That voice on the other end of the call can convince you to give information you typically would not give somebody. The incoming call will be designed to evoke an emotional response from you, whether that is a knee-jerk negative reaction or a positive emotion (whichever works in their favor).

For example, you may be offered a discount on your cable service or something along those lines. If someone called you and said you won a free cruise, you'd be deeply suspicious, especially once they started asking for personal information. But if it's a company that you do business with like Comcast, Verizon, AT&T, Time Warner, etc., your guard may not be on high alert.

I recently received a call from a number I didn't recognize, and when I answered, it was someone saying they were from Comcast and that they wanted to offer me a discount. Having just pulled this very trick on my friend, every mental alarm was going off, but I played along for a little bit. I have no idea if it was a scam or truly Comcast, but the individual was atrocious at talking—it was either his first day or he was an unskilled scammer. After the call, I Googled the number, and there were complaints about that vendor trying to sell people things related to other services. They may not have been straight-up scammers, but they were definitely doing some questionable marketing, and they were probably not directly affiliated with Comcast. This also triggered a memory I had of solicitors coming to my door a month earlier pretending to be with AT&T. They asked me about what Comcast services I used and said AT&T would be offered to me in the future. Could this have been related? I'm not sure, but that would be a lucrative way to scam people: visit them at their door, get them to answer a couple questions that they could then use to call you weeks later, and gain your trust quickly by pretending to have access to your account services or plan details. Then the customer might offer them one or two personal details, thinking they are legitimate.

Tip

Never give out any information at all when someone calls you.

Even if it is a payment or billing problem, simply tell them you will call them back and ask for their extension. Look up the phone number to the company online and do not trust one they may provide you. Not only will this help prevent you from providing information to an imposter, but it will also protect you against legal but illegitimate companies trying to get you to purchase their services. In some instances, it may be a charity requesting a donation but the charity, although it sounds worthy, is pocketing a majority of your donation. Illegitimate or unscrupulous companies or nonprofits like this usually never have a phone number that actually works when you try to call them, and simply Googling the name and number they provide will tell you whether you should call them back or not.

Donation & Nonprofit scams

When donating, ensure you're giving to legitimate organizations. Generally speaking, organizations that take donations are hotbeds for scammers. Even after natural disasters, you will see scammers pop up collecting donations when they have no affiliation to any legitimate organization at all. They could be a fake organization or pretending to be a well-known group. Never donate or provide any identifying details to someone that cold calls you. If you like what they have to say, go directly to that organization's website and donate. The worst of these crimes are when the victims of a disaster are targeted by scammers offering them relief, and instead they end up scammed.

Also, make sure to really understand the organization that you are donating to. Some organizations, although they seem like they're helping people, might not be a nonprofit. An interesting and popular example of this is the drop-off locations for things like shoes and clothes. Being that you see these often in supermarkets and retail areas, people trust them and drop off their donations. What many people don't realize is that you're not actually donating to something that you can write off as a tax deduction. You are just giving it to a company that then sells it for profit; they are not a nonprofit organization at all. Be aware and ensure you are donating to well-known and trusted organizations.

 **Remember**

Always do your research to ensure you are donating to a well known and respected nonprofit.

I recently received a cold call from the "Cancer Survivors' Association" that came from a phone number that had the same area code as my phone number. For most people, this will increase the likelihood of answering and help establish a little more trust rather than an unexpected or unknown area code. What immediately struck me was that I was on the Do Not Call list, and this call came to my cell phone. However, the Do Not Call list does not prevent nonprofits from calling you and asking for donations. Immediately thinking this was a scam, I began to gather information. They wanted my credit card number for a donation of any amount I'd like, or they could send me a packet in the mail. Surprisingly they knew my address without me telling them, but it was an older address I no longer lived at. When I asked them how they got my information they replied with, "We get contact information from multiple sources." Following the rule of never providing information on the phone (even though they seem legitimate and have my name, phone and mailing address), I asked for a phone number where I could call them back, and they provided one. When I called that number back it instantly played a message that "All representatives are busy, call back later." I called back and received the same message.

Next, I started to Google everything I could about this company and found that some people had already done quite a bit of detailed research on this nonprofit several years ago. It turns out the nonprofit was just a front for a legal scam, and that a majority of the money donated was paid to a call center company to cover the cost of fundraising. The website also looked like a scam (poorly designed with little content and no contact information), and there were no positive reviews about the nonprofit anywhere. It has been running for years and has collected millions of dollars from people. Even more astonishing is that there are several of these "nonprofit" associations that are all paying the same fundraising call center, a private company, which has made tens of millions off of donations to the organizations they service. This is legal, it works, and is very easy to fall for. Many stories of people who have "donated" did so because they know someone close to them which has been impacted by cancer.

 **Tip**

Never donate on an impulse, out of emotion, or on a cold call you receive.

In addition to calls, also be on the lookout for spam SMS or text messages. Never open any link sent to you by a phone number or email that you do not know. Sometimes, they will provide a phone number for you to call. Do not reply or call these unknown numbers.

Did you know?

▶ More than 86.2 million calls per month in the US are phone scams
▶ 1 out of every 900 calls to a financial institution is fraudulent
▶ 2.5% of US phones receive at least one robocall every week[26]

Spoofed phone numbers

A spoofed phone number is a phone call where the caller ID shows a number as one from which it is not truly originating. For example, I could call your phone from my phone and fake the phone number so that you think one of your other friend's phone is calling. This is incredibly easy to do and can be done by anybody, including you.

Resource: Caller ID spoofing

http://dsg.tips/spoof

This can be used to have a really great laugh with your friends and play a few pranks. It can also be used by ex-significant others and for other miscellaneous creepy and shady purposes. However, this can also be a strategic tool for hackers to fool you. A hacker can call you and appear to be from your cable company or your bank. The main point is, don't trust caller ID as a form of establishing the trust that the party calling is truly indeed that party.

Remember

Even if you trust a number that you think is calling you, stick to never giving out any information on that call. As recommended before, Google the number, call the company directly, and then resolve the issue.

Catfishing

Catfishing is when someone establishes a fake identity, usually to engage in a romantic relationship, and steals the target's money. There are many other permutations of catfishing—sometimes even the police employ catfishing to catch criminals.

Catfishing is sometimes done for revenge, out of loneliness or to steal money. Catfishing was popularized to the general public by the MTV show, "Catfish."

In summer 2015, AARP published a cautionary tale of a catfishing case that lost one woman over $300,000, in addition to serious emotional attachment. "Amy" was a widow in her late 50s who lived in rural Virginia, near family and close friends. She wasn't isolated, and she was tech-savvy: she had a website for her business, relied on her smartphone, and used social networks fluently. Reluctantly, two years after her husband's death, she ventured onto Match.com. One day she saw that she had a "100% match" with a man in his early sixties who lived in the same area – a stroke of good luck, it seemed. She messaged him first, and so began a romantic correspondence with a kind, imaginative man who wooed her with song lyrics and promises of a future together. He was hard to Google, with a cryptic LinkedIn profile and variations in how he spelled his first name: sometimes Duane, other times Dwayne. His accent, similarly, seemed to shift now and then. Regardless, she felt a real connection with him. They spoke every day, often for hours, and she had never met a man so curious about her.

Duane first asked for money for a work-related reason: he had plenty of funds, but cashflow was a bit tight, and he had to pay a customs fee. Then there were visa fees, and a few thousand dollars here and there to help him pay employees on time. At the same time, their plans to meet kept falling apart for reasons that remained murky to Amy. She joked to him once that she wouldn't be sure he wasn't a Nigerian scammer until they met face to face. Not long after that quip, Duane vanished.

With that, the spell broke. Amy, reeling, dedicated herself to finding out why. She did a reverse image search of a photo of him, and found that his name was not Duane or Dwayne at all; she wasn't even sure if the picture corresponded with the voice she'd been speaking with. When she told her regional FBI officer she suspected she'd been scammed out of over $300,000, he told her a woman in a neighboring town had lost over twice that much in exactly the same way. As it turned out, tracking down a skilled catfisher and returning stolen funds is nearly impossible. The financial and psychological tolls on the victim often linger for years.[27] Although catfishing victims usually don't lose this much, it demonstrates how powerful this type of scam can be.

You should take extreme caution when establishing new relationships with someone strictly via a computer. Using video chat to ensure you are talking to who you think you are can significantly reduce your chances of getting catfished. However, just because you can see them and they appear to be who they say they are, this does not mean that they may not be manipulating you to get money or account details out of you in the future.

In this chapter, we've covered some of the ways that web-based scams and attacks manifest themselves. In the next chapter, we'll turn to one of the key tools used by attackers and victims alike, a feature of our lives so essential that many of us interact with it several times a day and trust it with sensitive information: email.

FOUR

EMAIL

Importance of email security

YOUR EMAIL account is one of the most important things to secure. Not only is it a principal means of communication for most people, but your email is also used as a second authentication factor to reset your password on many of your other websites and accounts. Having complete control over someone's email gives hackers the keys to the kingdom. Because of this, be sure to use the methods described earlier in this book to ensure your account is secure. This includes two-factor authentication, using strong passwords, rotating passwords, and properly setting up forgot password questions, and backup methods like your phone number.

Your email contains a lot of personal information about you. Given access to your email account, someone could quickly create a list of most of the websites you have accounts on. They could identify which banks you use and your general spending patterns. They could see what websites you order from, what shoe or clothing size you wear, what electronics you own, and much more. Someone could identify your commonly used usernames on other websites and gather data on your friends, family, and coworkers. Many people don't realize what a significant amount of information can be extracted from the years of email history you probably have.

Email is one of the most popular ways that hackers use to infect victims and compromise businesses. It is extremely cheap to do at scale, and this can greatly increase their odds of success. If the company you work for has 100 employees, a hacker could cost-effectively target all the employees because they only need one person to make a mistake and let them in. Protect yourself and your company by learning to identify suspicious emails.

Email handling

Email attachments

Email attachments are a very common way that a virus or malware can infect your computer. In some cases, you will immediately see that the email is suspicious, but with a well-crafted email, it may not be so easy. It will appear to come from another employee in the company, it will be addressed to you and have your name, you may see your company logo and phone number on the signature of the email, and it may contextually make sense. For example, the email and attachment may be listed as "Yearly benefits updates" or "Q1 financial summary." Just because it looks like a PDF (.pdf), spreadsheet (.xls), or document (.doc, .txt, .rtf) does not mean it is safe. You especially don't want to open executables (.exe, .dmg) or zip files (.zip) but malware can be embedded in the most innocent-looking documents.

Tip

Play it safe and NEVER open an email attachment unless you were specifically expecting it from that particular person.

In fall 2009, multiple British police departments found their computer systems had been hit by a virus that encrypted their data and demanded a ransom to decrypt it. The virus found its way in via email attachments – which were opened by credulous employees. While most of these cases affected a few files on specific computers, the ransoms totaled thousands of dollars of public money spent to resolve a problem that started when someone opened an email attachment they shouldn't have.[28]

This cautious instinct should not only apply to your work environment, as you may also be subject to the same thing on your personal email. In some cases, the email may legitimately be coming from your friend or family members email address. However, it could be a virus, malware, or hacker that has gotten control of their account. It is so easy to open an attached picture from someone you know, and the hackers are betting on exactly that. Before opening anything you weren't previously expecting, contact the

sender via phone, text message, Facebook—anything besides email— and see if indeed it is legitimate. It may take
a few more minutes before you can view that attachment,
but it will save you days and a big headache if indeed it is
a nasty virus.

HTML emails

Historically, HTML emails were extremely dangerous to
leave enabled. Today, HTML emails are very common, and
there is little information available on the current risk of
such threats. If you are viewing your emails through a web-
based email client like Gmail, then you are probably safer
than if you use an email client that runs as a program on
your computer (Outlook, Thunderbird, etc). If you prefer
to be on the cautious side and don't have a need for aes-
thetically pleasing emails, set your email client to only view
plain text emails.

Tracking images

Many email clients, whether web-based or located on your
computer, have the option to enable and disable the automatic downloading of images. You may notice that when
viewing an email, you need to push a button to download
and display all images. Sometimes you can't even read any
of the email because it is made up of all images — this is
a technique to get you to load the images. Something that
you should know is that those images are being used to
track you as you open the email. They also track when you
click the links from within an email. If this email is coming
from an online store that you buy from often, this may not
be that big of a deal to you from a privacy perspective. But

if it is some sort of spam, loading the images will confirm your email has been read and gives them confirmation that your email is not only valid but that you will open these emails. This will result in significantly more unwanted spam. You should always set your client to disable the displaying of images at all times; unless you explicitly tell the email client to load the images for a particular email that you trust.

Spoofed email addresses

You may have encountered a spoofed email address, for instance when you receive an email that appears to be from an address of someone you know, or a company you know. However, it was not actually sent from the email address that appears in the "From" field. The proper way to check this is to view the headers of the email. This makes it a little bit more complicated for most people to identify an email's authenticity. If the email is asking you to reply with something and you click reply and the email address that it's going to reply to is different than the address the original email was from, that is a red flag. Another key indicator for these types of emails is that the To: line is empty. As I said earlier, if it feels funny then don't act impulsively: instead, investigate. You should never open any attachment sent to you by email unless you are explicitly expecting it. Just because it looks like it came from someone you know does not mean that it did. In many cases, it actually did come from your friend's email address—maybe even your friend's computer itself—however, that email could've been sent by a virus, and that attachment could be the virus trying to spread. Take a moment to think about whether it makes any sense at all that they would be emailing you this particular attachment. In our digital age, we crave the instant gratification and speed of operations that technology affords us, but the safe thing to do is to get in touch with the person who sent it, confirm what it is, and that they did indeed send that email.

Phishing emails

Phishing emails are one of the most popular tactics used by hackers. Being able to identify misleading emails is incredibly important for your safety and your company's safety. These emails will look like a legitimate email, usually from someone you know or do business with. An example would be an email from your bank asking you to log in and check an alert on your account — perhaps a possibly fraudulent transaction? Something that creates an impulsive emotion to click the link and log in as quickly as possible.

In January 2009, for example, Bryan Rutberg responded to an email that prompted him to click on a link to his Facebook account. The link took him to a site that was identical to Facebook's homepage, so Bryan quickly typed in his username and password. As it turned out, the site was a fake, and Bryan had just given an attacker his login details. Soon Bryan's friends were receiving messages saying he'd been robbed, and asking them to send money to a Western Union branch. One friend sent money; it was never recovered.[29]

When done correctly, these fake emails are works of art. They look highly realistic and do an excellent job of creating an emotional and urgent response from the recipient. This results in you making mistakes, like clicking a link in an email instead of going to the website directly, or not double-checking the URL of the website you are about to log into. Be aware that in many cases, simply clicking a link inside a phishing email is enough for the attacker to compromise, infect, or break into your computer — even if you identify it as fraudulent, don't click the link, not even out of curiosity. They might be trying to infect you by exploiting a bug in your browser instead of trying to get your bank details. By infecting your computer, they can take over all of your accounts, take pictures of you, steal or delete all your files, etc.

The number one easiest tip is not to click any link inside an email—ever. Instead, manually open a new tab and type in the URL yourself. If it feels funny or fake, try and validate its authenticity before you act. Never trust the contact details in an email either. You may be inclined to call the sender by dialing the phone number in the email, but instead, you should always go to their website by typing or searching yourself and then find their phone number. If you received an email to urgently call your power company to prevent interruption of service, you might call the large number right in the middle of the email. Once you dial that number, it is going to sound very legitimate and you will have no way to identify that it is a scam unless you catch them slipping up while speaking with them. Always get their phone number from the website.

Another indicator that the email may be malicious is if a link in the email has a target URL different than the text of the link. Don't click the link to figure this out; instead, you can usually see the destination URL when you hover over the link. If it doesn't match, that should be another red flag.

Remember

Avoid ever clicking links in emails unless you absolutely have to and you were specifically expecting it.

Many phishing emails use spoofed email addresses, addresses that appear to be from a legitimate source but are not. Sometimes they aren't trying to infect you or prompt you to call them, but rather they want you to open an attachment with a virus or, most frequently, get you to go to a website and enter login or security credentials of some sort. You might get a notification email that appears to be from Facebook, Twitter, or your bank, and when you click the link, the website looks EXACTLY how you'd expect, but if you enter your login credentials, you would be handing them over to the criminals. I have even seen examples where employees receive an email that there will be layoffs and they can view the severance package at the following URL. When they click, it looks like a legitimate internal company page but instead provides the logins to the hackers. The initial email was specifically designed to create a strong and irrational emotional response, causing people to act without paying attention to the small red flags.

Did you know?

► According to surveys of phishing in the first quarter of 2015, 59.2% of all email traffic was spam[30]

Common Scams

Many scams are still deployed through email. Two of the most famous are the penny stock scams and the Nigerian prince emails. Although these are well-known and have been around for years, there are still many scams being run that look similar to this – Bryan Rutberg's phishing experience was built on the advance-fee scam model, where a hacker asks the victim's contacts for one-off financial help. The reason they're still happening is because they are effective. These usually get people that are older and less understanding of technology, but they are always evolving. Here are some other scams you should be aware of.

 **Resource:** Popular email scams

....

`http://dsg.tips/emailscam`

....

Opt-out and unsubscribe

Be aware that any time you enter your email, you are most likely subscribing to some sort of newsletter. You may additionally be providing that company the authorization to send you emails in the future. Ensure whenever you order something or create an account somewhere that you read the text carefully about what you're opting into. Often the checkbox is designed to confuse you, so sometimes it needs to be checked to opt out, sometimes it needs to be unchecked.

Spam filtering has gotten significantly better these days, especially if you are using a free, web-based email service like Gmail. However, it is inevitable that you will end up subscribed to several legitimate mailing lists, and you will continually get a lot of email that is probably not that interesting. I recommend that you opt out of these. Again, you need to pay attention to the wording; you have to do more than just click unsubscribe. You then have to "confirm unsubscribe" after that. And that may only unsubscribe you from one of the multiple lists that they might have you on. You may have to select "unsubscribe from all." Some websites that are a little less scrupulous will require that you log into them to unsubscribe. This is a tactic meant to create more friction in the process.

Tip

Unsubscribing and streamlining your email inbox is important from a productivity and efficiency standpoint, so I recommend doing that from time to time.

Bottom line, pay attention when unsubscribing to ensure you have completed the unsubscribe process and opted out of everything you don't want.

You should also have a junk email account that you can use on less established websites or for registering on untrustworthy sites. Many websites these days will hide content behind a form where you have to submit your contact information. In some cases, this subscribes you to a mailing list or gives them permission to reach out to you and try to sell you something. A junk email is great for giving out in these scenarios. It is one you can still check, but don't use for anything of importance.

Another method you can use to help boost your email organization is Google's dynamic email aliases, if you use Gmail. If your email is johndoe@gmail.com, you can add a + followed by anything you want to the end of your username. For example, johndoe+mailinglist@gmail.com You could then use that email for all mailing lists. This makes it easy to set up filters for how those emails should be handled automatically. The best part is there is no prior setup required, you can just send an email to +anything and it will work. I don't recommend you use this to create a unique email address for every website as that would make your filters a nightmare to remember, especially on top of a good password strategy. However, there are special use cases where it can be useful.

Final thoughts

Keep your email client up to date! Ensure you have automatic updates enabled and check that your email client is regularly updating. This can prevent hackers that may try to take advantage of bugs or security holes in outdated versions from being successful.

Search your email account for the word "password." You may find old emails that actually contain your password in clear text. Permanently delete these if you find any — they should be extremely rare. Any website that can provide you with your existing password as a reminder is using outdated and dangerous security practices to protect your password. If you ever do a forgot password request, and they send you your current password (instead of a link to a password reset page), not only should you delete that email and flush it from the trash bin, but you should change your password on that website to a junk password. Additionally, delete any email you have from the past that you received with one of those reset password links in it. Although they should not work any longer, I recommend you clean them out.

Email can be a surprising Achilles' heel in many cases. In this chapter, we've reviewed the best practices for avoiding spam and viruses – thus saving you the frequent headache of wondering what to do with that barrage of questionable emails. In the next chapter, we'll open up to a bigger part of the security picture, and one that governs our real-world reputations: privacy.

HOW IS THE BOOK SO FAR?

If you like the book and are finding value in it, please show your support by sharing and helping to spread the word about the Digital Survival Guide on Facebook, Twitter (@dsgbook), LinkedIn, or any other social network you use. This small action makes an enormous difference and I greatly appreciate your support.

http://dsg.tips/share

If you are not happy or don't believe it is worth sharing, please reach out — I want to hear any feedback you have. Only with your feedback can I make the book better. Please reach out at:

http://dsg.tips/feedback

I also encourage you to provide feedback about sections you like or dislike and any comments you may have. Thank you, and read on!

FIVE

PRIVACY

Why care about privacy?

PRIVACY HAS become a hot topic in the past couple years, especially with recent events like Edward Snowden's leak of government documents exposing the mass surveillance of citizens. In today's digital age, there is a massive amount of data about us — everything we do, everywhere we go, whom we know, talk with, etc. Most of the time people don't think about the fact that data is being collected about them or how that data can be used.

There is so much data about our lives being recorded. How are we as consumers expected to be able to know everything that is being collected and how it is being used? Unfortunately, there is no clear answer to that, and in many cases trying to deal with it just leads to mental fatigue. Most people will end up saying, "Whatever, I don't really care," or you will hear the rather sanctimonious statement,

"I don't have anything to hide." If you are one of these people, hopefully you will reconsider after reading this chapter and have a better understanding of the magnitude of how privacy is changing in the digital age.

I have come up with specific questions you should be asking or thinking of when it comes to your personal data privacy. By answering these questions, you can make an educated decision as to whether you agree or disagree with a company's data collection about you. Based on that, you may choose to stop using a particular company, service, or product. However, you will find that it is nearly impossible to answer all these questions accurately. It is a bit of an alarming notion. Here are the personal data privacy questions:

- ► What exact data are they recording or saving?

- ► Is the data anonymized, or is it linked/identifiable to me?

- ► How long are they keeping that data for?

- ► What is that data being used for?

- ► Who has access to that data?

- ► Is that data being sold, or could it be sold or shared with another company in the future?

To be clear, engineers usually want more data about you — the more data about you, the better. It means they can create more targeted types of products and services. The government wants this data to reduce crime and help with criminal investigations. (There is plenty of angry rhetoric around this, but I'm working under the assumption that the government isn't an evil empire trying to steal away our rights and impose a police state.)

What is tracked physically?

Let's take a look at some ways that your physical location could be tracked or is currently being tracked today.

If you drive a car, most intersections and freeways have cameras. Do you know everything those cameras are used for? Since you are in public and have no expectation of privacy, they probably have legal grounds to automatically read your license plate number. If most intersections you go through and freeways you drive on have cameras, and they were to log the license plate, time, and location of every car that passed, they could instantly look up your typical driving routes and routines. From a technical perspective, this is something a college-level software engineer could implement. If your local county or state began this type of operation, they probably wouldn't make a public announcement about it.

We know the video from those cameras is being recorded, but for how long are those recordings kept? If they chose to begin recording license plates, times, and locations, they could go back through the archived video and identify every time your car shows up in the past. This could be years of information about you if they keep the video for that long. Maybe they only keep the video for 30 days, but if they decided to keep it forever moving forward, it's not likely they would notify you with a letter in the mail...

Some might feel violated by this, and some might be saying, so what? There are perfectly legitimate reasons to collect and use this data: identify perps from a crime, track illegal activity, optimize roadways and traffic lights for better predictable traffic flow, etc. However, before you could make a decision about how you feel on this, you should understand the answers to the personal data privacy questions presented before. You know they could hypothetically track your license plate (tied to your identity), location, and the date and time your vehicle was seen. Let's assume they will save the data for 90 days and it is primarily used by law enforcement to solve crimes and the transportation department to improve traffic. Let's also assume that access to the data is limited and has a lot of oversight to prevent fraudulent access or abuse of the system. Finally, assume that they will not sell the data or share it with anyone else. Given all of these perfect-world conditions, it may not sound as scary. However, the reality is a bit more complicated.

That data could still be acquired through court orders or warrants. Also, is the data being secured properly to prevent hackers from stealing it? If they changed their policy on how long they will keep the data for, how will they use it? If they now want to sell or share it, would they tell you and if so how? Finally, even if you are comfortable with it today, what prevents them from using that data in the future in a way you may not agree with?

Imagine if one day you woke up and were able to search anyone's name in your city and see their driving route and where they have been any day for the last several years because some hacker stole all the data and leaked it on the Internet. Alternatively, could this data be used against you? Could a court subpoena this data and attempt to use it to establish a characteristic or generalization about you? Say you were involved in a traffic accident where someone was injured or killed. Could they use historical data showing that you sped a lot in the past to prove you are a reckless driver and possibly at fault for this most recent incident?

Many major cities provide electronic devices you can place in your car to do fast payment through toll areas. These are also used for commuter lanes as well as parking garages. In the San Francisco bay area, this is called Fas-Trak. Every time you cross one of these sensors, a transaction is created and tied to your identity. All data about you is deleted approximately 4.5 years after it was generated. Even if you close your account, your history will remain. Additionally, at toll crossings, they will also automatically read and record your license plate number and save that transaction the same way even if you don't have a FasTrak device. Luckily they have a very clear Privacy Policy that lays out what they track, how they keep it, and who they share it with. Check it out as a good example and perhaps look into the privacy policy of what is being used in your area:

Resource: Fastrak

http://dsg.tips/fastrak

If you think that it is only those cameras and toll payment devices tracking your every position, then the rest of this chapter may deepen your concern.

Today most people carry a smartphone. Have you ever looked at your notification screen on Apple's iOS or Google's Android phones and noticed it says how long for you to get home or to get to work based on current traffic conditions? The interesting thing about this is, you never told your phone where your home is, or where your work is for that fact. So how does it know this? Your phone has been using your location information and monitoring it over time to understand where you spend your nights, aka home, and a general pattern of where you spend your days, aka work. It is probably also aware of when you usually leave your home in the morning and when you normally leave work. Even if you turn GPS off, they can still do reasonably accurate position tracking using only wifi. The feature itself is really useful, and you might be in favor of trading in that privacy for convenience. However, let's not make that trade-off without asking our personal data privacy questions.

- ► Is that data only being collected/monitored on the phone itself or is that data being sent back to their data center for analysis?

- ► Is it anonymized if sent to their data center?

- ► How long do they keep that data if they do send it to the data center?

- ► Are they using the data for anything else?

- ► Are they selling or sharing it with any other company?

- ► Additionally, you might want to know:

- ► How often are they checking your position? Every minute? Every hour?

- ► When did I consent to them collecting or monitoring that data and using it to generate insights? You most definitely did — their legal teams ensured it, I promise you.

Both Apple and Google have worked towards improving user privacy & security, especially with recent leaks of government data collection programs. But without an official statement or security research firm investigating, we simply don't know the answer to all these questions. It seems surreal that a company could be collecting data about your location every 10 minutes and storing that for extended periods of time completely legally and without you knowing. With that type of data, I know where you sleep, where you eat, where you work out, where you work, what friends you hang out with, and what time you do all of these things and how long you do it for.

These companies have the capability to collect your GPS position data in conjunction with the wifi networks that your phone detects constantly. When this is done with millions of phones, they are able to use those wifi networks to calculate more accurate position information of all smartphones. This is how your phone can determine your position even if it cannot get a solid GPS signal. This is why you see the warning on your phone that you can increase position accuracy by enabling wifi. This begs the question though, if they are collecting this data from you, are they saving this data tied to you or your phone's identifier, or is it anonymized? We'd like to think it is anonymized. According to Apple's Location Services support page,

"If Location Services is on, your device will periodically send the geo-tagged locations of nearby wifi hotspots and cell towers in an anonymous and encrypted form to Apple to augment Apple's crowd-sourced database of wifi hotspot and cell tower locations."[31]

If you had some clever remark going through your head about how this is why you don't use a smartphone or don't use location GPS and wifi, think again. All cell phones, even non-smartphones, keep in touch with cell phone towers, so they know where to route an incoming call. Because the signal will hit more than one tower, your position can actually be triangulated from the signal strength and timing of your cell phone's check-in with the towers. Personal data privacy question time: Is this information recorded? How long is it kept? Who has access to it? Who is it shared or sold to?... you get the idea.

During the Edward Snowden exposures, we heard the words "metadata" being repeated over and over — the NSA claimed only to keep your phone number, the destination phone number, and time and length of the call. Technically the signal strength and time that your phone checked in with the towers is metadata as well. Even if the telecom companies aren't sharing it with other companies or the government, we should know whether they are even recording it to begin with and if so for how long. This means Verizon, AT&T, and other major wireless telecom providers that control the cell phone towers could know all the same things that smartphone OS providers know about your position, just by collecting position data through a different medium. For that fact, anyone (or company) could set up monitoring stations and track this data to pinpoint your position. Granted, they would have to link your phone's identifier to your identity since they wouldn't have access to that data like your telecom provider does. Wireless telecom companies just happen to have a nation- (and world-) wide network with strong coverage already in place.

A company called Stingray created a fake cell phone tower product that allowed them to track the position of users cell phones by pretending to be a cell phone tower. Several police departments have started using this and considered buying it, as have some federal agencies. However, there has been a significant amount of backlash, since using such a device does not require a warrant and is seen by many as an invasion of privacy.

With cars getting more sophisticated and integrating more advanced technology, it opens the opportunity for your car manufacturer to collect position and driving data about you as well. If you car has an onboard GPS, they could collect data about your driving habits and location. This data could then be used to improve the experience of driving the vehicle, add features to your driving experience, or it can be used when your car experiences problems to send diagnostics to the manufacturer. Sounds pretty cool, but again raises all the core questions. You'd probably never realize if car manufacturers started doing this and you'd have no idea how they stored the data or who had access to it. With new cars like Tesla having an always-connected 3G connection, your car's exact position could be tracked by the telecoms as well as your car's manufacturer (and perhaps even police agencies using devices like Stingray). Even the popular OnStar service has been known to track and record your position.

We just identified the following, highly realistic and probable ways your location can, and in some cases is, being legally and precisely tracked.

1. Public cameras that could track your car at intersections and on freeways

2. Toll, parking, and commuter lane electronic payment/identification devices

3. Your cell phone OS, which is currently tracking your GPS/wifi position to some extent

4. Your telecom provider that currently knows your position via signal strength to cell phone. And possibly people using devices like Stingray to pretend to be a cell phone tower.

5. Your car manufacturer that could be tracking your position through your in-car GPS or always on 3G connection

We don't really have clear insight into who is exactly recording what, but we know it is entirely feasible from a technical standpoint. We also know we have signed away our legal right to privacy with many of these companies. Most of the contracts and terms you sign in the purchase of a new product or service have broad sweeping clauses that give them the right to collect whatever they want about you and do whatever they want with that data, including sharing or selling it. It is also important to consider that if they aren't doing it today, might they have the right to do it in the future without explicit consent or notification?

 **Tip**

Be on the lookout for when companies you use are acquired or sold. When a company is bought or sold, so is your data.

Looking past your cell phone, there are other physical technologies you use that can leak a lot about you, beyond just

your location. Think about your credit card or bank transaction history. They have your transaction data that can
give insights into your physical location, spending habits
or budget, brand affinities, and a lot more. One of its best
use cases is to detect fraud when your card is stolen and
attempted to be used somewhere else, where you are not.
They can also use that data to derive advertising insights
about products and services (theirs and otherwise) that
you may be interested in. But all the same personal data
privacy questions still apply and cannot be easily assessed.

Unfortunately, there isn't much you can do to protect
yourself from all this possible data collection except for
dropping off the grid and I'm definitely not recommending that. I do believe though that by becoming aware of
what could be collected, we can open this privacy topic
up for discussion. Once we start seriously discussing this
type of tracking as a society, the general public can create
pressure for companies and our government to do more to
protect this type of data, be transparent about collecting,
and be honest about what they do with it. They may also
be forced to stop or allow users to opt-out. By heightening
your awareness on this topic, hopefully the next time you
see a request for support or data privacy issue arise in the
media, you will take a little extra time to pay attention to
what is actually happening. There are privacy advocates out
there digging deep into these issues and putting your best
interest first, but they face big money, lobbyists, and the
status quo, and they need you to stand behind them and
show your support. Do your homework before making a
stance, but my hope is next time you will be a little more
conscious of the issues at stake than before. If you have an
interest in getting more involved with these conversations,
then check out the resources I have put together.

Resource:
Get involved with privacy rights

http://dsg.tips/getinvolved

What is tracked digitally?

When it comes to browsing the Internet, your privacy is significantly more compromised than you realize. Beyond cookies, which we cover in detail later, there are several other ways to fingerprint or uniquely identify you. Honestly, no one knows more about what you do on the Internet than Google. A lot of Internet browsing starts with a Google search. After you search, they track each website you go out to. However, Google also runs the largest online advertising network in the world where they display ads on a vast number of websites across the Internet.

Additionally, they also have one of the leading, free website analytics and tracking tools. This allows people who run websites to get free analytics data about their users — how often they return, how long they stay, where they do or don't click, etc. If you visit a website using Google ads or Google analytics, they can track that you were there, even if you didn't get there from a Google search.

However when you pull together your searches on Google, plus websites you go to that are using Google analytics, and websites that use Google ads, a detailed picture emerges. Google has a pretty good idea of almost every website you visit, how long you stay there, and how many pages you view. Not to mention things you searched for... think about what it would look like and what you could learn about someone simply by looking at what they have searched for in the last year. Google has a general "Don't be evil" philosophy, but as we continue to make trade-offs between privacy and convenience and improved experiences, the line of what people are okay with is changing. You may not mind that Google uses this data to provide more relevant ads to you, but you may mind if that data was made public. What if you somehow got sued or had to go to court and your search and browsing history was subpoenaed? Or what if your search history was stolen by hackers? Granted, Google spends enormous amounts of money on security — but if a hacker was targeting you directly and was able to access your Google account, they can request your entire search history to be sent as an archive to your email which they could then download. If someone was out to smear you politically or publicly, they might give this a shot.

Many people don't know this, but there is a page you can go to on Google that will show you details about your search history and browsing behavior. It is interesting to check out and it may encourage you to turn off some of the optional tracking about what you do on Google. Check it out for yourself:

Resource: Google history

http://dsg.tips/google

You will also find additional information at the link above on how to change your privacy settings to reduce the amount of data that Google is recording about you. Additionally, Google takes a look through all of your email on Gmail in order to target advertisements for you.

There are hundreds of other advertising and analytics companies out there that are tracking everything they can about you. We now see a huge amount of websites sporting their Facebook and Twitter social tags. These are also used to collect more data about you. You can see nearly 100 companies in the NAI (Network Advertising Initiative) that track information about you that you can opt out of. Here is a guide I recommend you check out to reduce the amount of tracking that is done to you online.

Resource:
Reduce tracking of you online
....

`http://dsg.tips/stoptracking`

....

Your ISP, Comcast, AT&T, or Time Warner (or whoever provides your Internet) can also see a significant amount of what you do on the Internet. As we talked about before, you should be using SSL as much as you possibly can as this makes the contents of the sites you visit hard to read by middlemen like your ISP. However, when you type yahoo.com into your browser, your computer goes to your ISP and asks them to tell your computer the IP address of the domain yahoo.com. This is called DNS resolution and can give them enough information to see where you are going and when. Are they keeping that data? If so, for how long? How is it being used and accessed? You get the idea by now...

If you are tech-savvy and would like to change your DNS provider (it won't significantly increase your privacy, but can slightly increase your Internet speed and reliability in some cases), check out this tutorial:

 Resource: DNS optimization

`http://dsg.tips/dns`

Even if you opt out of tracking cookies, block tracking cookies, and clear all remnants of tracking data in your browser, you can still be reasonably identified (beyond using your IP). The technique is called fingerprinting and is done by identifying unique subtleties of your browser and system information. To see how unique you appear on the Internet, check out this tool:

 **Resource:** Fingerprint your browser

`http://dsg.tips/fingerprint`

Other monitoring techniques

Your cell phone and any device with wifi has a unique hardware identifier called a MAC address. By passively monitoring this, you can learn a lot about someone like when are they home, or when they normally use their laptop. This static unique identifier could be used to track your behavior. This isn't just a theory: I have seen an R&D project that did precisely this, and there are even retailers that at one point had a similar system implemented, like Nordstrom. There are interesting benefits for retailers or other businesses to identify your cell phone upon entering the store. For example, they can get insight into business metrics like how often customers are returning, how long they stay, and where they go in the store. However, customers are being tracked without their knowledge simply because their phone has wifi on and that results in their presence being unknowingly announced.

In some cases, the wifi device – often your cell phone — will send a list of SSID's (names of wifi networks) that you have connected to previously out into the world around you. It is called a probe request, and if one of those wifi routers is there, it will respond back to your phone, so your phone is always saying, "are any of you out there?" This doesn't sound like a big deal, but by seeing a list of networks you have connected to, I may be able to determine your name, gender, recent hotels or vacations you may have been on, where you work, what conferences you may have attended, and what coffee shops you may have visited. It is a significant amount of information that can be derived from data you had no idea your phone or laptop was just sharing out there on your behalf. It is an invisible sphere of personal data that emanates from your mobile phone.

There have been recent improvements to help mitigate this. Some devices, like iPhones, now use a random
and rotating MAC address. This prevents your device from
being tracked by people simply listening in and seeing
your device communicating with a wifi network or trying
to communicate with a wifi network in your surrounding area. Additionally, many companies have limited the
broadcasting of the SSID's or the names of other networks
you have connected to. Although this threat may not be as
large of an issue anymore, this was happening, and people
were collecting this data for a while. You never realized it
was even happening. It shows how easily personal information about us can be leaked and tracked without our
knowledge.

Protect your privacy

Hopefully, thinking about a few of the things you use daily
and how they can be exploited for good and bad gives you
a bit more suspicion about the technology around us and
how it can be compromising our privacy. As consumers,
we need to start asking the core questions to our technology and service providers. Right now, customer support and
sales representatives usually have no idea about what their
own company is really doing with your data — by voicing
these questions, we can ensure companies are transparent
and can clearly communicate their data policies.

Remember

We have to apply pressure to ensure we get transparency and answers about the core privacy questions.

There are many ways to increase your privacy, especially online but also in the physical world as well. I have put together an up-to-date page with some of my favorite as well as popular tools in the industry. It is a pretty extensive topic but worth checking out if you want to do more to protect yourself.

Resource: Privacy tools

`http://dsg.tips/privacy`

SIX

PUBLIC RECORDS

Types of public records

W<span></span>E LIVE in an age where it is easier than ever to discover information about you. The interesting thing about public records is that there are a lot of them out there about you that you may not even know exist. Some of these are what I call semi-public records; for example, voter registration information. These can be requested and acquired by political organizations, but the general public doesn't have access to them. This doesn't mean anyone can't get their hands on them, but it is just harder for the general public to do so. Ghost, the hacker interviewed by VICE who was quoted in the social engineering chapter of this book, told the reporter that publicly listed addresses are often his first source.

Beyond that, many records are entirely public. For example, your mortgage and property purchase leaves public records online. Deaths, foreclosures, civil court cases, and bankruptcies can all leave additional public records out there about you. In today's Internet age, dozens of companies have looked to making a profit off of public records by collecting, aggregating and making those records searchable.

You might find that your name, phone number, email, and previous addresses are being listed on dozens of aggregator sites. Many of these sites do allow you to request your information be removed – but this can be onerous and time-consuming. I recommend you take the time to clean them up though. To make this easier and automated, you may want to check out this service:

Resource:
Cleanup your public information

`http://dsg.tips/public`

Not only can people use these public records to learn more about you, but they can affect your credit or be used by insurance companies. Unfortunately, it is nearly impossible to get most public records removed, but by removing yourself from aggregator and background-check sites, you can make the information exponentially harder to track down.

Mugshots and Arrest records

Mugshots.com and jail.com are the largest in this genre right now. For a list of websites that should be checked and cleaned up if you have ever been arrested for anything, see here:

Resource: Mugshot websites

`http://dsg.tips/mugshot`

Google, MasterCard, and PayPal have taken steps to stop supporting mugshot-type websites due to their blackmail type tactics. However, you may find some websites are still doing this. If they are attempting to profit from your name and image (i.e. make you pay to remove your photo and information), then you may be able to have it removed without paying. See the resource above for more details.

Mitigating public information

Unfortunately, you don't have many rights to have public records removed from their official sources. In some situations, you can have court cases sealed if you were a witness or juvenile, but it is best to speak to a lawyer about this. However, if you do find a court document related to you that contains your social security number, birthday, bank accounts, or children's names, you should contact the court about getting that information redacted, as that is your right.

Search for yourself

One thing you can do is to search for yourself on the Internet. Search for your first and last name and then add your middle initial, then your entire middle name. If you have a popular name, you may want to include the street name or city you have lived in before. Additionally, search for your current and previous addresses. You can also search for current and old phone numbers as well as your email address. You may also want to search for usernames that you have used. You might be surprised by you find. Be sure to look at multiple pages of search results — someone looking to find out more about you will probably go several pages deep, if not look through them all.

 **Tip**

If your email or phone number are showing up, you may want to investigate each of those results as they may have a way for you to remove that information (and you should). At the least it will help reduce spam email and marketing calls.

When searching for your name, you should also check Google images to see if there are any pictures of you that show up. I also recommend that you do these searches on other popular search engines like Bing, just to understand how you appear online. Your appearance when searching for your name is important, and you can help curate that experience to be more favorable. For example, if you have ever been arrested, chances are your mug shot is public information and may show up on the first page. By properly setting up your Facebook, LinkedIn, Twitter, etc., you can fill the top results up with more ideal results and hopefully push any unwanted results off the first page.

Remember

Searching the Internet for yourself and your image is something that you should do during your yearly digital checkup to see if anything new has popped up.

If you use one of the services I recommend for automating the cleanup of your public information, they do offer ongoing monitoring and automatic removal that may interest you:

Resource:
Cleanup your public information

`http://dsg.tips/public`

The information in this chapter is drawn from common-sense approaches to keeping your reputation clean online. More than ever, we Google people we know or are curious about: job applicants, dates, etc. It is important to take charge of your own reputation online, and to know your rights in terms of curating those results. In the next chapter, we'll turn to optimizing your everyday digital experience – starting by opting out of those tedious marketing lists, and extending to potentially malicious communications.

SEVEN

OPTING OUT

Direct mailing lists

W E ALL get too much junk mail every single week. We take it out of the mailbox and promptly dump it into the recycle bin. The amount of mail that comes through our mailboxes and directly into the trash or recycling is a waste of resources. Most people I know won't open anything that doesn't have their name on it. Ads or envelopes addressed to "Current Resident" go directly into the trash unopened. However, there is a way to unsubscribe from some of these to help reduce the amount of junk you get. Not everyone honors this unsubscribe request, and they are not required to by law, but it is worth being proactive. There are also a couple of companies that are helping people to unsubscribe from unwanted snail mail. I maintain a list of current resources for opting out and automation of this here:

Resource: Opt out of direct mail

`http://dsg.tips/optoutmail`

Prescreened credit offers

Prescreened credit card offers are mainly sent to you in the mail. Once they get hold of your information, they just keep on coming. Sometimes it is surprising how they get your information, but nevertheless, they do. Many tasks like simply buying a new car can result in public information, or your information being sold to marketers. They will then try to sell you extended warranties or other offers they think you may be interested in. It is all a very shady and persistent market. Generally speaking, never apply for a credit card that is sent to you in the mail. You can go online and find great credit card sign-up bonuses.

The good news is, some of these prescreened offers come from companies that respect your ability to opt out. To opt out and stop receiving some of these, go here:

Resource: Opt out of credit card offers

`http://dsg.tips/creditoffers`

Do Not Call Registry

You can opt out of many marketing phone calls by entering your number into the National Do Not Call Registry. I highly recommend you do this for all of your phone numbers in your family. You can do so here:

Resource:
Opt out of marketing phone calls

http://dsg.tips/donotcall

If you're not sure if your phone number is on this list, it's very easy to go to their website and check. This will not stop those calls altogether, as some companies are going to call illegally. Some companies will use loopholes or other borderline-legitimate ways to call you. In these cases, you will need to opt out individually. If it's an automated system, usually they tell you what number to push to opt out. If it's a real person, tell them you want to be placed on their do not call list and that you want your number removed from their database. I usually take a friendly approach for first-time offenders. Being a jerk isn't going to encourage them to cooperate.

Robocalls

Some marketing systems use prerecorded voices that sound real. This should raise a red flag immediately if there's anything odd about the timing between when you talk, and they respond. If there are awkward silences and the phone call fluctuates between normal and abnormal, then there's an issue. If you suspect this, I recommend you ask a question challenging it, to see if they're human. A good example would be, where did you get my phone number from? Or, what company are you calling from? Also, companies calling you about credit, debt or mortgage, should be instant red flags.

Remember

When in doubt, ask them for their business name and a phone number where you can call them back.

Most illegitimate companies don't have a way for you to even call them back. Once you have a name, the number that called you from caller ID, and the number they gave you, a few minutes on Google will give you a clear picture of who these people are and if they are legitimate.

Remember

By simply avoiding giving out any information on phone calls that come to you, you will be significantly more safe. Yes, from time to time that will mean the inconvenience of having to hang up, searching online for that company's phone number, and then having to call them back. It is worth it.

In this chapter, we went through the ways you can fend off unwanted intrusions before they happen: by opting out ahead of time, and knowing how to react on the spot. In the next chapter, we'll move beyond those key aspects and into another everyday essential of life in a digital age: how to securely browse the Internet.

EIGHT

Securely browsing the Internet

Using a trusted computer

USING PUBLIC or shared computers is generally a very bad idea. This includes Internet cafes, libraries, business center computers in hotels, etc. When using one of these computers, you have no idea what security protections, if any, they have put in place. Do they keep the computer up to date? Anyone can plug something into it or download a virus. Or people may go to an infected website without knowing and infect the computer. Do they run a virus scanner? You get the idea.

Unless you are in a situation where you absolutely have to use a public computer, then don't. If you do, and you have to access something like your email, I recommend doing a password change from a trusted computer as soon as possible afterward. Be sure that when you are done on any website, you log out. I also recommend you use the browsers private or incognito mode to help isolate your session and reduce remnants you may leave behind, like history and cookies.

You may find yourself at an event where they provide laptops for people to register or sign up with. In these scenarios, when registering, I'll use an insecure junk password and change it later. If I'm ambivalent about what I'm signing up for but doing so is required anyway, then I will probably use my junk email address as well.

Cookies

You have probably heard about cookies before — they are small pieces of data that a website can store on your computer. Anytime you visit that website, it will see that you have this cookie from a previous visit. Cookies are mainly used for identifying your session, i.e. if you need to log into the website, they already have a unique identifier that tells them who you are and that you are already authenticated. If someone got hold of that cookie, they could browse around your logged-in account as if they were you; this is called session hijacking. Some websites will limit how long your session is valid for before you have to log in again, usually banks and other financial institutions. Other websites, like social networks, will allow you to stay logged in forever, as long as you go to the website from a computer you have logged into before. It will send your session identifier and you don't need to log in again or do anything else.

A second principal purpose of cookies is tracking. They are used to store an identifier on your computer that can then be read as you browse around the Internet. This links your activity across many websites. You may notice that you view an item on Amazon, and then you see ads for that item on other websites. That is because Amazon placed a tracking cookie on your computer so they could do precisely that. Many companies do this, mostly for advertising, but there are other analytical use cases as well.

If you'd like to increase your privacy and reduce the amount of tracking done on you, I recommend you check out these browser plugins:

Resource: Cookie blocking

`http://dsg.tips/cookies`

Additionally, if you are interested in reducing the amount of advertising you see on the Internet, there are several great ad-blocking add-ons for your browser. See my recommendations here:

Resource: Blocking ads

`http://dsg.tips/ads`

Super cookies

Super cookies aren't talked about much, and most people aren't aware of them. There has always been debate around the privacy implications of cookies and the lack of regulation around using them to track people. Cookies are an accepted method of tracking despite being questioned and scrutinized by privacy advocates. Super cookies, however, use more aggressive and unorthodox methods, and many major companies avoid using them. They are still in use by a handful of organizations, though.

So, what is a super cookie? It is a unique identifier that a website stores on your computer, but it not only stores it in a normal cookie: super cookies can use over a dozen other methods to store and later read a unique identifier on your computer. It is incredibly difficult to block and remove all these identifiers once they have been placed on your computer. Even if you delete most of them, all it takes is one lingering trace, and when you visit a website that uses these super cookies, they will immediately and forcibly all be repopulated from the one identifier you neglected to remove.

If you are interested in learning more technical details about super cookies, check out this additional information:

Resource: Super cookies

http://dsg.tips/supercookies

Using a secure connection

If you don't know what SSL is, it is when you view a website using a HTTPS URL instead of a HTTP URL. The difference is subtle but incredibly important. Modern browsers also show a SSL banner to help you clearly identify when you are using SSL. When browsing the Internet and not using SSL, there are a few things that can happen. First, anything you request and anything you submit or send can be read by anyone. This includes someone eavesdropping on the network or shared wifi network you are using, your ISP, the government — anyone. By using SSL, they can still see where you browse on the Internet. The secure connection will, however, encrypt the contents of your communication: the content of the page, your credentials, etc.

The second issue is that, without SSL, it is very easy for someone to perform a man-in-the-middle attack. This is where your connection is routed through a malicious computer in-between you and the intended website. With a man-in-the-middle attack, the contents of your request or the website can be altered without you knowing.

Third, if you log into a website or browse a website while logged in without SSL, they can take your unique session identifier from your cookie by eavesdropping on the network, place that cookie on their computer, then use their own browser to go to that website and the website will assume it is you. They would have full, logged-in control over your account.

Tip

Never log into a website that isn't using SSL/https.

Another important tip with SSL is to ensure that you are not just using SSL, but that you are using a valid SSL certificate. You will know when you are not, because the browser will display a warning screen that some aspect of the SSL certificate is not correct or trustworthy. If you choose to accept this invalid certificate, you could be subject to a man-in-the-middle attack where someone between you and your desired destination is decrypting your communications and possibly modifying them. Here are some ways to validate your SSL connection and identify when you should not accept or continue:

Resource:
Validate you're securely connected

http://dsg.tips/ssl

Shared Internet connections

It is best to always use a trusted Internet connection, ideally your secure, private, home Internet connection. However, this cannot always be achieved and sometimes you may have to use public wifi at coffee shops, airports, etc. When using an untrusted Internet connection, you should employ extra due diligence to ensure the websites you are visiting are using SSL. I also recommend you avoid logging into anything unless you have to — I never recommend you log into bank accounts or do anything financial while using shared Internet connections.

Use an abundance of caution when not using your own Internet or an Internet connection you trust, like a family member's. Even when using a friend's or family member's Internet, you most likely don't have any idea about the security of their network and computers — keep that in mind. If their wifi does not have a password, then you should refrain from using it, as there is a much higher likelihood of someone lurking and waiting for an opportunity.

People love nothing more than some free wifi Internet, and that includes hackers. When you connect to these free and open wifi networks, hackers can use an array of tricks to make your computer connect to theirs as you browse the Internet. This is that man-in-the-middle attack I described before. In some cases, this not only results in your browsing being watched, but they can use it to take full control of your computer by intercepting and injecting malicious code into the web page. Avoid public and free wifi. It is safer to use your phones 4G or LTE connection.

Remember

Make sure your home wifi is secured and not open to the public.

Additionally, make sure you are not using WEP (wired equivalent privacy) as your wifi router security mechanism and instead ensure you are using WPA (wifi protected access). Also, if your router supports WPS (wifi protected setup, a short code on the router designed to make connecting easy for users), then you should log into your router and disable it.

Did you know?

► 80% of households still have their wireless routers set up with default passwords[32]

I also recommend that you log into your router and update the router firmware — not only could there be security fixes, but performance and reliability fixes as well. I had a friend complaining about slow Internet connectivity, so I checked out her wireless router. It was a hand-me-down from her brother, and the firmware (the software that runs the router) was over a dozen versions old — from 2005, with the most recent version being from 2013. After updating, not only did it patch some minor security issues, but her wireless Internet is now running significantly faster. For a tutorial on how to update your wireless router, see here:

Resource: Update wireless router firmware

http://dsg.tips/wireless

Validating a websites' legitimacy

From time to time, you may find yourself on a less-established website. Maybe you are trying to buy something that is rare and unique and not sold by major online retailers. Before you provide them your username, password, email, and credit card information, take a moment to ensure they are legitimate. Are they using https with a valid SSL certificate? Google the name of the website to see if you can find additional material about them. I also like to add the word "review" after their domain name, i.e., "store.com review," to see if I can find other people who have ordered from them and reviewed their experience. You can also use the word "scam" to see if people have had experiences where they got ripped off from that website.

Watch out for typosquatting. This is when fraudsters register a domain with a common missing or extra character, or a frequent misspelling of a popular service. They then set up a page that looks exactly like the original website. However, when you try to log in, they capture your details and then can steal your account. If you ever fall victim to a scenario like this, where you log in and then realize the website is not the real website, get to the real website as soon as possible and change your password.

Dialogs, extensions, and autocomplete

Trick dialogs

From time to time, you may see a website displaying a dialog or visual of some sort, appearing to be a dialog your computer or operating system would display. It makes you think something important is happening with your computer, browser, or another program on your computer. You should beware of these techniques as they are designed to make you click on the important-looking dialog. Since these fake dialogs have malicious or unsavory intent, it is crucial you understand how to spot them. The best way to protect yourself is to know what types of things to look for. I keep an updated list of examples at the following resource.

Resource: Trick dialogs

http://dsg.tips/dialog

Browser Plugins & Extensions

There are three broad categories of browser plugins and extensions we need to address.

1. Standard extensions that enable functionality on the Internet: Adobe Flash, Adobe Acrobat Reader, Microsoft Silverlight, Oracle Java, etc.

2. Browser extensions you intentionally installed.

3. Browser extensions you did not intentionally install.

For group number one, these provide you with a lot of functionality when browsing the Internet. For example, many video players on the Internet rely on Adobe Flash.

However, these extensions have been notorious for having bugs that would allow an attacker to infect your computer by simply visiting a website. Some people think they are safe because they only go to a few trusted websites, but hackers will often find a way to get the infection onto one or more pages of a trusted website. Adobe Flash has had over 50 severe bugs in 2014 and over 75 in the first half of 2015. Acrobat Reader had over 30 in 2014 and 50 in the first half of 2015, all considered severe.[33]

There are dozens of other known bugs. I hope these facts highlight the importance of keeping your browser on automatic update and never putting off the restart to update dialog request.

A great way to protect yourself from attacks through these vectors is to disable automatic plugins running in your browser. You can then enable them to always run on sites you truly trust. Although this may require you to manually activate the plugins on some sites, it is significantly safer. Especially since malware attempting to infect your computer may not even be seen on the page, so you are less likely to activate the hidden troublemaker. For a tutorial on how to do this and what your experience will be like after doing so, see the following article:

Resource:
Disabling browser extensions

http://dsg.tips/ext

For group number two, extensions you did explicitly install, these should be fairly safe, especially if they are well-known extensions with hundreds of installs and reviews on the extension marketplace. If you don't use extensions or have no idea what these are, they provide additional features to your browser and are developed by a third party. An example would be an ad-blocking add-on for your browser. Although these are usually safe, do keep in mind they can access quite a bit of the browser, including all of the websites you visit. They could transmit all that information back to their servers, so just be careful and choose well-known plugins.

For the final group, extensions you did not explicitly install, these are fairly common. Either the extension was installed via some malware or an infected website you may have visited, or it could have been installed as part of installing some other software (they usually allow you to opt-out, but that can be easy to miss). When you notice an extra toolbar on your browser, or your search results suddenly going to a new search engine, or any other unexpected sort of behavior starts happening in your browser, then you should investigate. Look at all the extensions installed on your browser and disable any that you do not know. Not only will this help protect you, but it will also make your browser operate faster and smoother.

Browser Password Managers

Do not use "remember my password" in the browser. You should also refrain from using all the autocomplete fields for credit cards, name, and address. These are just another vector for hackers to attack when trying to steal information about you. They have been exploited many times in the past and been known to have security issues. It is just best to avoid using them. Ideally, you should use a digital wallet to avoid storing that information on your computer in any program.

Mobile Apps

The most recent way to access the Internet is through the booming industry of apps, especially mobile apps. It seems like every company has an app these days, and your financial institutions are no exception. However, after reviewing the research on the security of financial institutions' apps, I have uninstalled all of them from my phone. Seriously, the number of security holes found in mobile banking applications is very concerning. If you do have mobile banking apps on your phone, then limit their use strictly to your home and trusted wifi network. Using a mobile banking app on an untrusted network like in a cafe is extremely dangerous; don't do it and limit your use of banking applications in general.

Did you know?

▶ 40% of banking apps tested in 2014 did not properly ensure a secure, encrypted connection with the bank[34]

If you are interested in the more technical details and research around the security holes in banking and mobile applications in general, check out this article:

Resource:
Security vulnerabilities in apps

http://dsg.tips/apps

Terms of service

Clicking Accept without reading

We are all guilty of this one, and who could blame us? Those terms or use/service are excessively long and filled with legal mumbo jumbo that we don't fully understand. Also, it isn't like we have a choice to negotiate the terms — we either accept the terms they are forcing us into, or we don't get the product or service.

However, every time you click "accept" you may be signing away more rights than you thought, especially when it comes to privacy of your data and your ability to defend yourself if your privacy is violated. There are a couple of websites that help make these long terms of service easier and faster to read. To check out the most popular ones, check out this guide:

Resource: TLDR terms of service

http://dsg.tips/tos

What you usually agree to

Many websites and services make you agree to some pretty unsavory things:

- ► They have the ability to use your content (posts, pictures, etc.) however they want, which includes selling or licensing it to other companies.

- ► When you close or delete your account, they can still retain rights to the data you put on there when active.

- ► They have the ability to track and store data about you, including but not limited to your usage and behavior. In some cases, this includes not just their website but also any of their partner or affiliated websites.

- ► They can change the terms at any time without notifying you.

- ► They can delete whatever they want, your data or account, at any time for any reason without notification.

- ► When you delete data, they retain the right to keep the data for whatever reason they want.

- ► You waive your right to sue or join a class-action lawsuit against the company.

These are just the major points, but there are dozens of caveats depending on the type of service. It gives them ultimate protection and takes away most of your rights to control your content, privacy, and ability to hold them responsible for anything bad that happens. Seems fair.

Hopefully the industry will come up with a way to help standardize these terms of service and define what is generally accepted by consumers and what is unreasonable. Unfortunately, we don't expect to see that happening anytime soon. There is little public outcry calling for it. Mainly, people don't read them, so they don't even know. Like security, it is a second thought until it becomes an issue.

Remember

Terms of service are legally binding contracts.

In many cases, you agree to their terms of use, acceptable use, and privacy policy simply by using their website or service. For example, you agree to all the terms from Google by doing a Google search.

Licenses and other legal agreements

When installing software, you also agree to a license agreement. These usually cover all the same terms and also include a few more to cover the illegal distribution of the software. Keep in mind that just because it might be a desktop or phone app, the makers still can, and do, collect a significant amount of data about how and when you use their product. This includes data you may store in that application.

In this chapter, we covered the logistics of safely browsing the Internet. We also zeroed in on the process of downloading from the Internet and signing up for new services – something that, as the programs we use proliferate, will only increase in frequency in the future. In the next chapter, we'll go one step further: we'll delve into how you can proactively secure and back up your digital documents.

NINE

Digital documents

The cloud

There are many different definitions of what the cloud is, but generally speaking, it refers to a method of storage where data is stored in a data center rather than locally on your device's hard drive. In many use cases, the cloud has become synonymous with syncing, as in your data is backed up in the cloud and will thereby stay in sync on all your devices. This allows you to access your content or data from any device or computer, from any location and at any time, even if all your devices are destroyed.

This makes your data and information safer from them being lost or destroyed. A very common use of the cloud is to store a backup of your photos and contacts from your mobile device. This way if you drop your phone into a lake, you can quickly and easily get back up and running.

In September 2015, photography site PetaPixel reported that a Des Moines, Iowa, photographer lost six memory cards containing thousands of photos from over 20 wedding, family, and newborn shoots – as well as two laptops and her wallet — after her car was broken into. Like most of us, the victim kept the memory cards in the same bag as her valuable equipment. The photos were not backed up, and a $5000 reward was posted for information leading to the thief's arrest. For the photographer, it was a nightmare: she had to call each client and break the news that they would never receive professional photos of an event that was important to them. For the clients, it was worse: some ended up without a single photograph of their wedding day. Uploading the images to the cloud as soon as possible would have saved both parties a great deal of trouble.[35]

Although this illustrates the advantage of using the cloud, it does open you up to new attack vectors, a.k.a. new ways for your information to be leaked or hacked. An attacker no longer has to break into your physical device to get your data, pictures, or whatever else they might be interested in. The hackers only have to get into your cloud account. If you are not using two-factor authentication and are using a weak password, this can make your data much easier for them to break into. Make sure any service you are using that stores your data is protected by two-factor authentication.

You are also trusting the companies you share data with, your cloud providers, to protect you. These are usually large companies, and they take customer data, privacy, and security very seriously. But the more data a company has about people, the higher their value as a target. These companies are constantly being attacked, and there have been cases where even the most secure companies have been partially compromised.

Remember

Many "cloud" products do not encrypt your data, or they encrypt it after it gets to their system.

If you want to be safe when using the cloud or a backup solution, your data should be encrypted before it leaves your local device. This is not just while the data is in transit, or while stored on their servers using their encryption keys — this is where it is encrypted using your password or key and can only be unencrypted by you. Most solutions do not provide this level of encryption yet, but we may see more providers moving towards solutions like this. There are important caveats, however, to data encrypted by only a password you have; mainly, this data cannot be recovered if you forget your password.

Using the cloud can be very convenient and beneficial. Ensure your account is secure with a strong password and two-factor authentication if possible. Also consider removing items from the cloud that could be sensitive or compromising. Celebrities have had nude or personal photos of themselves leak because they left those photos synced in the cloud and probably had less than ideal account security in place.

Backing up data

Although many people consider cloud syncing their backup strategy, it is actually a very risky thing to rely on. If a hacker gains access to your cloud account, they can delete all of your data from all of your devices. Because of this, I recommend you enable two-factor authentication on your cloud account. This might be Apple's iCloud, Google Drive, or your Dropbox account. This can help limit the ability of a hacker getting in and deleting everything or resetting your devices.

If you are serious about protecting your data, I recommend you follow the 3-2-1 backup rule. The 3-2-1 rule of backups is universally accepted as the recommended guidelines for personal data backup. This 3-2-1 rule is also recommended by the US-CERT (United States Computer Emergency Readiness Team):

- ► 3 – Keep 3 copies of any important file: 1 primary and 2 backups.

- ► 2 – Keep the files on 2 different media types to protect against different types of hazards.

- ► 1 – Store 1 copy offsite (e.g., outside your home or business facility).

So let's dive a little deeper into what it means to have three copies of every file.

The first copy is the primary copy on your computer hard drive that you already have and use today.

The second copy is a backup to a local external device. This external device could be a hard disk, thumb drive, network drive or Apple Time machine. This copy is mainly designed for fast backup and restore. It serves as an alternative to your third backup copy.

The third copy is a backup to an offsite location. This offsite backup will usually be done using a backup or cloud provider of some sort.

My personal recommendation is to take it a step further and to make your second copy an offline copy, not just a local copy. What I mean is, I recommend you backup to your local external device, and then physically disconnect it from your computer or network. Doing that can provide you with additional protection from a hacker who may have gained access to your system and prevent them from wiping out your backup. Additionally, it can help protect you from ransomware, a nasty new malware that encrypts all of your data and forces you to pay a ransom to get it back.

Remember Mat Honan, the technology journalist from Chapter 1 who was hacked because someone else wanted his neat Twitter handle? He lost over a year's worth of documents and photos of his young daughter from his Google and iCloud accounts. Had he been following the 3-2-1 backup rule, he would not have suffered such a disastrous loss.

 **Tip**

Use an automatic backup strategy that syncs to a data center and follow the 3-2-1 backup rule!

Personally, I limit the amount of data I allow to sync between all my devices to what I essentially need or might be working on at the moment. I then use backup software to encrypt the remainder of my data and send only an encrypted copy to a data center. Then once a month I connect an encrypted portable hard drive, take a backup of all the data I sync out to the data center/cloud, and then store it away in a fire-resistant, water-resistant safe. It is important not to leave the device plugged in, as a hacker could wipe the device if they were to break into your computer. You should also encrypt the data in case the drive is stolen or seized. And storing it inside a safe is just a good idea if you have one.

Remember

If your data is maliciously deleted, there is a close-to-zero chance that you will ever get it back.

A cloud or a sync storage utility will protect you in the event of a device theft, malfunction, and some hacks. It will not protect you against a hacker deleting all the files in the cloud or sync program. You may also be vulnerable to ransomware. Those pictures of your friends, family and children, the digital receipts and tax documents you have to keep in case you get audited, all those other papers and documents could be deleted forever. For my current recommendation of the best products, check here:

Resource:
Backup product recommendations

http://dsg.tips/backup

Encrypting data

Encryption is vital to protecting yourself in a digital world. Encrypting your data can prevent it from ending up in the hands of a thief if your device is stolen. It can also prevent police or investigators from using your data against you in the unlikely event you find yourself in such a situation. It can also keep your data secure when backing it up into the cloud. It is a best practice to use encryption and one you will need to embrace. For a tutorial on how to enable encryption on common devices, see here:

Resource: Encrypt your devices

http://dsg.tips/encrypt

Take a moment to check if your mobile devices support any form of encryption or data protection and enable it. Many phones come with this enabled by default, but don't assume — take a moment to check.

Apple uses FileVault for encryption on their computers and prompts you to enable it when first setting up the computer. Windows uses Bitlocker and starting with Windows 8.1 it is on by default.

Securely deleting data

Many people are not aware that when they delete something from an electronic device, it doesn't truly delete the data. For example on your computer when you delete a file, it is not removing the actual 1's and 0's from the hard drive. Instead, your computer keeps an index, a list of all files and where on the hard drive each file can be found. When you delete something, your computer simply removes that index. Sometime in the future, the actual data might get overwritten since they are not marked as being in use by the index list. However, it is possible for it never to be overwritten.

Using a special piece of software, hackers can scan the hard drive to try and identify these files that haven't been overwritten but have been marked "Deleted". When you use a computer to do your taxes and store other financial information, simply putting the file in the recycle bin or trash can and then emptying it is not enough. There are a few ways to handle this. On a Mac you can use secure erase by dragging the items into the Trash, and then choose Finder > Secure Empty Trash. Using Secure Empty Trash takes a bit longer than simply emptying the Trash. If you are using disk encryption, you can set it to automatically overwrite your deleted files.[36]

For Windows you will need to install a third-party program to securely delete files. For my recommendations, see this resource.

Resource: Secure Delete

http://dsg.tips/delete

If you are selling your computer, you should either remove the hard drive and sell it without it, or format the hard drive. If you remove it, you can find a local recycle center that does shredding and ask if they have a hard drive shredder. If you decide to format it and reinstall the operating system, you can run a program to overwrite all the data on the hard drive to ensure your old data cannot be recovered. The way this data is usually deleted is by writing random ones and zeros (or all zeros) over every data location on the storage device and sometimes doing so multiple times to ensure that there is no remaining data. Then a fresh install of the OS will make it back like new. For details on how to do this, check out this tutorial:

Resource: Format your devices

http://dsg.tips/wipe

If you are encrypting your hard drive, which you should be, then this makes things significantly easier. Because the old data is encrypted, you wouldn't necessarily need to write zeros over the entire hard drive — but it can't hurt to do so if you have the time. Note, if your computer has an SSD hard drive, you may want to ensure you are using the correct tool to format it. SSD drives can be "reset" in a way that erases all the data on the drive without having to write 1's and 0's over the entire thing. This is more efficient than how it use to be done with spinning magnetic hard disks.

Remember

The same types of data recovery attacks can be used to recover your data from any form of digital storage. Keep this in mind before discarding mobile phones, digital cameras, tablets, memory cards, etc. Using a trusted e-recycling provider, especially if they have specialized shredding machines to destroy media like hard drives, is recommended.

Don't forget: if you were using a backup strategy or cloud syncing strategy, there may still be traces of that document lurking around. This may be fine if you want to keep an archived copy; however, if you are truly trying to destroy or erase the existence of a document, it would be fruitless if your cloud or backup tool kept a copy in the "trash" forever.

In this chapter, we covered how you can be proactive in securely saving or deleting your data. In the next chapter, we'll cover the other analog parts of your digital life: the papers, cards, and records that support our everyday transactions, but that could also be the target of identity theft.

TEN

Physical documents

PROTECTING PHYSICAL documents is just as important as protecting digital documents. Your physical documents can be easy to acquire, sometimes without your knowledge of them being stolen. Sometimes it is as simple as losing your wallet. Those physical documents can then be used to steal your identity or ruin your digital reputation. In this chapter, we'll go through the most important physical documents to keep safe.

Pickpocketing

Everyone is vulnerable to pickpocketers, especially when traveling abroad. Although you can easily start to protect yourself by not leaving your wallet or cell phone out on a table while you eat, pickpocketing can be hard to defend against. Many pickpocketing operations are run by multiple people. Sometimes the theft involves several people as a distraction, one person to do the pick, one person to create a visual shield so no one can see the pick, and a person to hand off the picked item. Even if you think you felt someone pickpocket you, the item could be handed off so fast that you won't be able to catch the person with your item or even know who has it.

We'd all like to think it won't happen to us, but the fact is that many of these people are professionals; pickpocketing is an art. They are skilled at focusing your attention where they want it, getting close to you without setting off your inner guard, and ensuring you don't feel a thing.

Remember

Your awareness of being pickpocketed is significantly lower than you think.

It is not as simple as keeping a valuable item in your front jacket pocket or front pants pocket; yes these are harder to pick than your back pocket, but not by enough of a margin to truly protect you. To understand the art of pickpocketing, you should watch the videos linked below. They are pretty amazing and will change your appreciation of how skilled these individuals can be:

Resource: Deception experts videos

`http://dsg.tips/pickpocket`

Now that we've established a suitable level of respect for the game, here are some things you should do to help protect yourself.

If you see a sign that says "beware of pickpockets," fight your instinctive urge to check your valuables. Pickpockets will often stand by these signs so they can see what pockets people pat down, showing them exactly where they keep their valuables. Also, try not to compulsively check for your goods every few minutes, that will provide intelligence of their location to thieves.

Avoid looking like a tourist, as tourists are the main target. When using public transportation, try to move as if you know where you are going. Don't carry a map in your hand.

If you find yourself in a crowded area or on public transportation, and you are suddenly closely surrounded by 2 or 3 people who have enough room to stand elsewhere, you are probably about to be pickpocketed.

Situations where anyone bumps into you, even if the context makes it appropriate (someone stops abruptly in line, or on a crowded subway car), should alert you. Also avoid commotions or becoming distracted by public scenes, fights, and street performances.

Backpacks and purses are great targets for thieves, as you won't feel them opening or a hand going into the bag. Try to keep them in front of you and use luggage locks.

Beware of snatch-and-grab thieves. They will usually give up quickly, but they will target people holding phones in their hand or bags where the straps can easily be ripped or cut. Some will even try to slash the entire bag open. There are slash-proof bags you can buy to help protect against this.

Be cognizant of your surrounding at all times. Thieves will target people who are distracted, absorbed in a device, or visibly drowsy.

Tip

Beware of anyone who approaches you asking questions, carrying a map, clipboard, or asking you to look at something or hold something (even a baby). This is one of the most common distraction methods.

Heavy coats and clothing are more likely to disguise the sensation of a thief dipping into a pocket. Keep items in your most guarded pockets, and during high-risk moments like in crowds or public transit, keep your hands in or covering your pocket.

Using a money belt is a good idea, but don't let it give you a false sense of security. Thieves can still get into them without you realizing it.

A pickpocket won't look like a thief. In some cases they might be kids — if you get swarmed by kids, beware. Kids have been known to crowd subway platforms and grab wallets as people push through them. Entering and exiting public transportation is overall one of your highest-risk times.

Make your items difficult to get to and try to keep your hands free as a defense mechanism as much as possible.

If you inevitably do get pickpocketed, just be sure that you didn't keep all your money and cards in one place. Ensure you don't keep important documents in your wallet. Know exactly what you will do (backup cash, calling card, etc.) if you do get pickpocketed. This will ensure it is more of an inconvenience with a minor financial loss than a major issue.

Protecting your Wallet

Your wallet carries a lot of personal information about you, and you may end up losing it once or twice — or having it stolen off a table or by a pickpocketer. Wallets that are physically stolen usually have the credit card numbers used immediately — within the first couple hours at nearby locations. In the event your wallet was stolen, are you prepared? Do you know what numbers to call to cancel your cards, or were they all on the back of the cards that were just lost or stolen? Once you have determined your wallet is probably not going to be recovered, you need to call your bank and credit card companies immediately. To be able to do this quickly, you should add the phone number from each of your credit cards to your cell phone. There is usually one specifically for lost or stolen cards, but the general customer service number is just as good.

 **Tip**

Save your credit card phone number to the cloud so you can retrieve it easily from another device. I recommend using Evernote or Google Docs.

When someone steals your wallet, they may hang onto your ID to use themselves or to be sold. A criminal may use it to pretend to be you if they get in trouble with the police. This is why you should file a police report if it was stolen — it will make clearing up any later misunderstandings significantly easier. I also recommend you keep a photo of your driver's license on your phone, in the cloud, printed and locked up, or memorize your driver's license number. These can make police more lenient if you were driving and forgot your wallet.

Extensive identity theft can result from a wallet being taken and exploited by a determined fraudster. In fall 2012, the FBI released the story of a Florida highway patrol trooper who thought he was looking into a simple case of driver's license fraud – but then it turned out the man, now imprisoned, had been using a living victim's identity for over 20 years. Starting with a car break-in and stolen wallet, the victim, "John Doe," had been living a bureaucratic nightmare. The perpetrator, who still insists the identity of John Doe belongs to him and claims to be the real victim in the case, used the identifying cards in the wallet to amass a stack of government identification: birth certificate, social security card, passport, and fingerprints when he was taken in by the police after a fight. He had even passed the background checks to get a special permit that allowed him access to military ports and installations. "He appears to have manipulated the system with ease," said a Special Agent working on the case. A jury convicted the man to ten years in prison, but he still has not made any admission of guilt.[38]

Do not keep your social security card, birth certificate, or passport on you. If you have a Medicare card, carry a photo of it and block out your social security number (ideally by placing something over it before making the copy). Also do not carry a spare key — after all, if you lose your wallet, your address is on the front of your identification card. Even if that address is outdated, they may be able to find public records using your name to find your current address. Do not carry personal checks or checkbooks.

Did you know?

► Leading up to the 2012 Olympic Games, there were 1,700 reported pickpocketings a day in London alone
► Most pickpocketing goes unreported to the police.[37]

It is a good idea to insert a business card or some sort of contact card — make sure it says that you are the wallet owner. You can also include an emergency contact on it, just in case your wallet is found by a good Samaritan.

You may be inclined to carry your health insurance or prescription cards. You should only carry these if you absolutely need to — like when visiting a new doctor or pharmacy. I recommend you take a picture of your prescription and health care insurance card and just keep them on your phone, that way it is protected by your password. Some people think they need to carry their card in case they have to go to the ER and are unconscious. However, hospitals will take care of urgent matters and ask about your insurance afterward. Worst-case scenario they will bill you, and you can then file a claim with your insurance company to get the money back. However, if you have the pictures on your phone, it wouldn't even come to that. I also recommend you add that you are insured and the group # to your phone's Emergency Medical ID info. This should be enough for them to locate your insurance while you are unconscious. You can also leave a copy of your insurance card with your emergency contact, so when the hospital reaches out to them, they can provide it. The security advantage of this one is clear: you don't want anyone else claiming your health insurance or trying to fill prescriptions under your name and account — leave 'em out.

Remember

Don't carry more cards or personal identifiers than you absolutely need to. Be intentional so that anyone who steals your wallet doesn't get more than the bare minimum; it will save you time and trouble.

Gift card scams

Gift cards are popular gifts, but are they really safe to use? In recent years, there have been many attacks against gift cards and gift card related scams. Here is what you should know to protect yourself.

When purchasing a gift card at a retail store, thoroughly inspect the packaging. If the protected scratch-off area has been altered or the wrapping material has been torn in any way, do not purchase that card. If you can see the PIN number in any way, do not purchase that card. Cardboard covers are more susceptible to tampering than plastic shells. Also, don't pick a card that just hasn't been tampered with, but pick one that is harder to get to — not at arm level, and not right in the front.

Criminals will try to copy the card's information, especially right before a gift-giving holiday season. Then right before the holiday, they will check the card's balance online, and if it has been purchased, they will go spend the card. When your friend or family member goes to use it, they will find the balance empty and probably think you were a real jerk for giving them an empty gift card.

Tip

If you insist on buying gift cards for the holidays, order them online instead of in a store to be safer.

Many gift card scams are perpetrated by employees in the store, sometimes the cashiers. If they ask you to scratch off the protective cover over the PIN number on the back of the card, you should refuse. Try and get their name from their name tag and report them to the manager.

When selling a gift card online, ensure you never give the PIN to a potential buyer — wait until the transaction has cleared. They may try and ask for the PIN so they can check the card's value, but once they have that PIN they can use the card without paying you. You won't be covered by traditional credit card liability protections, which means you probably won't get your money back if your gift card number and PIN are stolen. Definitely be skeptical of buying a gift card on auction websites where you deal with the buyer directly. Ensure they have several credible reviews and stay away from any seller with a negative review. Also, stay away from people selling anything at a significant discount or in bulk.

If you are going to sell your gift cards, I recommend you do some research and ensure you are only using a reputable secondary gift card marketplace. For my recommendations on where to sell your gift cards and make some extra cash, see this article:

Resource: Giftcard secondary markets

`http://dsg.tips/giftcard`

Identification Documents

Your social security card or anything else with your social security number on it is very important to protect, as it has become the US government's main identifier for an individual. I'm shocked that many people don't realize they need to protect their social security card. Many people carry the card directly in their wallets. This is one of the worst things you can do. If you don't have your social security number memorized — it is only nine digits — do so now.

A Forbes feature from 2014 profiled Amy Krebs, who took proactive steps to protect herself when her credit card was compromised. She called the three credit bureaus, only to find that the thief had already called them to rewrite her security questions and override her real identifying information. The thief had gotten hold of Amy's former address, maiden name, and social security number, and used that information to open over 50 credit accounts and to cover medical bills. Amy found herself pursued by collections agents, bounced from one government agency to the next, and consumed by the time-intensive process of filing affidavits and working with law enforcement to regain her identity. "It's the most time-consuming, upsetting, emotional event you have to go through," Amy said. She recommended asking twice before giving out your social security number next time someone asks for it. "Question when someone asks you for your SSN," she urged. "I'm shocked by how often, when I ask, 'Do you really need that?' they say no."[40]

Your birth certificate is similarly important. Generally, it is only required for other life-defining government filings, such as getting married. Know where it is and that's it's secure —preferably in a safe – at all times. Rose Vargas of Queens, New York, was unpleasantly surprised when she and her fiancé went to apply for a marriage license in 2004. The application was rejected on the grounds that she was already married. Not only that, but she was already married twice: once in Mexico and once in Ecuador. Rose's birth certificate had been lost when she was sixteen, and because it proved she was born in the US, it had been used multiple times in a scam to convince men abroad that they were marrying an American citizen and would thereby gain the right to immigrate. Fortunately, a judge was able to annul the bogus marriages, and Rose could at last proceed with her life – though she later learned her identity had been used in a third marriage scam, this time on Long Island. Once your identity is on the market as a commodity available for illegal purposes, it is very difficult to completely recover it.[41]

If you have ever lost your wallet or do lose your wallet with your social security number in it, you are at major risk of identity theft. Your driver's license plus social security card are the keys to the kingdom in many cases. I don't even recommend you store a digital picture of your social security card. Keep your physical copy at home, ideally in a secure safe or hidden location. Also do not carry your social security card with your passport or when traveling.

Passports are also important to keep safe. There are additional concerns with passports, as some passports have an RFID transmitter in them. This allows the passport data to be digitally scanned when the passport nears the customs agent's machine.

Remember

Criminals can make similar scanning devices, much like they can do with NFC (near-field communication) in credit cards, and steal your passport just by standing next to you.

You should generally never carry a passport with you when you're in the US. Always use your driver's license or another identification card instead. When you do take your passport out of your home, I would advise you to get a passport RFID cover to prevent people from stealing your passport information without you even knowing. Here are some recommendations:

Resource: Passport RFID covers

http://dsg.tips/passport

Your driver's license is a more complex case. You should carry it with you at all times for identification. However, a driver's license does have your name, date of birth, address, and driver's license number on it. Your driver's license number itself is not something you have to be as protective over to the same extent as your social security number. But I also wouldn't give it out or list it publicly.

A surprising quantity of important paperwork can be completed with a stolen driver's license. In fall 2006, for example, Anndorie Sachs received a phone call informing her that she was under investigation because her newborn had tested positive for methamphetamines. Anndorie was taken aback: a mother of four who was enrolled at the University of Utah, she had not given birth in quite some time, never mind the meth. Child Protective Services did not believe her denial: they interrogated her as well as her employer, family, and even her children (though they did not take the step of doing any DNA testing to confirm whether or not Anndorie was the mother of the newborn in question). Eventually, Anndorie was able to connect a car break-in from the past few months with the situation. A pregnant meth addict had stolen her driver's license and used it as identification through the hospital birth process – she had even put Anndorie's name on the birth certificate. Though the investigation against Anndorie was mercifully called off, she was left with persistent calls from the hospital to pay her $10,000 bill for the birth; all this because her driver's license ended up in the wrong hands. [42]

In the event that your driver's license is lost, you should report it and order a new one. If you move, you are supposed to write an updated address on the back, but any time I've been pulled over by the police, they have asked if the address on the card is current. If you have annoyed the officer, they might cite you for not filling in the updated address. But from a security perspective, it is not a bad thing that someone who steals your wallet can't get your current address by simply looking at your driver's license.

When your driver's license expires, you should be sure to dispose of it properly. I recommend that you put it through a shredder that is designed for properly shredding a credit card. Simply throwing the old card in the trash without fully shredding the card is risky. In addition to criminals, juveniles are also attracted to driver's licenses, even expired ones, as they may try to use it to buy alcohol or avoid being identified by the police if they get into trouble.

 **Tip**

Write or engrave your driver's license number onto your physical belongings. In the event they are stolen and recovered, the police can find the rightful owner. Additionally, many pawn shops will not accept items with someone else's driver's license number etched into it. Using a driver's license without any other information (like your name) is ideal for this purpose. The criminals won't be able to look up who the number belongs to, and the ID number will directly link it back to your identity for the police.

Securing your documents

When it comes to storing your important documents and valuables, you have several options. You could use a safety deposit box at your bank, but I have a few warnings about that. First, if you have a safety deposit box with a bank, beware that the IRS can freeze access to or seize that box using a federal judgment. This can be the result of a nasty tax situation or could happen due to a case of identity theft. This may not be as much of a concern if you are only storing documents, but if you are storing other valuables, you may want to consider using a private vault or safe company.

Second, if you ever receive a notice that the bank will be moving your box but you don't need to do anything, go and take all your items out until after the move is complete. There is a significant increase in things getting lost or mixed up during these moves. I was quite surprised with how many reports I found online of people complaining that items were missing or their box had been given to someone else after a move.

An alternative to using a safety deposit box or private vault would be to invest in a safe for your home. A safe is an investment and not the type of purchase where you should just pick a cheap model off the shelf. Practiced thieves have found easy ways to open these cheap safes in seconds. When choosing a safe, there are a few factors you should take into consideration.

What is the rating of the safe? There isn't anything that can't be broken into, given enough time and the right tools. That is why safes are rated based on how long they take to break into (this is usually done by a third-party company). A safe without a rating is much less trustworthy. A good safe will be labeled with a TL rating (TL-15, TL-30, etc.).

Is the safe fire-rated? If you are protecting documents and other valuables you will want to ensure the safe is fire-rated. Fire ratings are also usually tested independently and labeled as Class 350 1-hour, Class 350 2-hour, etc.

Is it water-resistant? Although you may not be in a flood zone, there are still many scenarios where your safe may take on some water unexpectedly.

Does it have holes and equipment to be bolted down? A safe is no good if it can simply be lifted up or put on a dolly. You will need to bolt it down to keep it secure.

Also, check for a UL rating; this is a rating from Underwriters' Laboratories. They are a non-profit, non-biased agency that tests and rates the safety and performance of consumer products of all sorts, including safes. For my recommendations on different levels of safes, see this article.

Resource: Safe recommendations

http://dsg.tips/safe

Shredding documents

Properly disposing of documents is just common sense. It is a simple step and adds a lot of security value. Shredders are relatively cheap and easy to find. There are a few things you should look at when purchasing a shredder, and the most important is the cutting pattern. You don't want a shredder that does only the long horizontal cuts to the page — the ones that look like spaghetti after being cut. With the use of technology, this limited shredding method has become even easier to reassemble by simply placing the strips on a transparency sheet, scanning them on a flatbed scanner, and using software to help restore the pages. It is a lot of work and something your common trash diver wouldn't mess with, but for just a few extra dollars you can get one that cross-cuts. Even better, find one rated for micro-cuts.

A shredder that cross-cuts will cut both vertically and horizontally, resulting in a small, confetti-like output. This becomes significantly harder to put back together. Another feature that you may be interested in is the number of pages you can put in at any given time, especially if you have a lot of shredding to do. You may also want one that can handle staples and paperclips without breaking. Many of them come with CD or credit card shredding slots as well. I highly recommend you dispose of old CDs you burned of your data by running them through a shredder that was designed to handle a CD or DVD. The credit card shredder will make it safe when you throw away old credit cards, business cards, driver's licenses, etc.

You should additionally shred all of your mail. Anything that has an account number on it or anything besides your name and address — and even then, you should consider shredding it. In an apartment, condo, or shared complex, your trash is much more susceptible to being looked through. I recommend that you shred everything, including the envelope, not just the part with the account numbers. If you have your own trashcans instead of shared bins, this is even more important — that envelope or generic page inside the Internet bill can provide information about the service providers you use. That can be used to manipulate you during a fake call or email. This definitely signals a higher level of security, but since you are already shredding the papers inside, why not just shove the entire thing through the shredder?

If you live in a city, then you have seen people go through trash; they are usually collecting bottles and glass for recycling. However, it is important to remain alert and ensure you stop anyone you see taking anything else out. Your guard may be down because you don't think they have the tech-savvy skills to steal your identity. You may be right, but an identity thief can offer to pay good rates for particular types of documents. So if they are in the trash and happen to find tax documents, anything from the IRS, or a page that happens to have a social security number on it, they can save it for the identity thief. This one find can earn them a week's if not a month's worth of trash-diving income. For my current recommendations on shredders, see:

Resource:
Top shredder recommendations

http://dsg.tips/shred

Limiting physical documents

I recommend reducing the number of physical documents that you have to deal with in general. Every time you have a physical document mailed to you, you are exposing yourself and your information to additional risk. Plus, for each new document you get in the mail, that is one more thing you have to shred. An easy solution is to enable the electronic statements on all of your accounts. Additionally, when receiving things like your tax refund, I do not recommend that you have a check sent to you, but instead opt for a direct deposit.

Regarding documents you are saving for tax time, I also recommend you convert those to digital. For things like bank statements, simply download them monthly or at the end of each year, and store them in a properly secure (encrypted) folder that is inside your data backup strategy. For things like receipts, I recommend you use a receipt-scanning tool and keep backed-up copies. This is safer, as you do not have your financial documents and history at risk of being physically stolen or lost in a fire. For my recommendation on receipt-scanning and management apps, see here:

 Resource: Best receipt scanning apps

http://dsg.tips/receipt

Limiting the risk to your physical documents will also mean less clutter for your home – a win-win! In the next chapter, we'll move from paper to hardware: how to protect your devices themselves.

ELEVEN

Physical devices

Keeping up to date

Th<small>E BEST</small> way to keep your devices safe, even better than using a virus scanner, is keeping your software up to date. Make sure your operating system has automatic updates enabled and be sure to manually check it from time to time to ensure it is working as expected. This is also crucial to do for your browser as well — infecting your computer with malware by exploiting your browser or a plugin your browser uses is one of the most popular approaches for hackers. Ensure you have automatic updates turned on for the browsers you use and again, manually check them from time to time. Don't stop there, though — go through all of your major applications and find the update settings. Your email client, Adobe Reader (what you use to view PDF's), Flash (mainly the browser plugin), and Java (mainly the browser plugin) are all primary targets. Not all applications support automatic updates or will even notify you. These updates could contain security patches that could prevent you from becoming a victim.

If you are more serious about increasing your safety on the Internet, I recommend that you disable the plugins in your browser so that they have to be manually activated when you want to use them. This mainly disables Flash and Java, which have been responsible for many computers becoming infected in the past. For a tutorial on how to do this and what it does, visit this resource.

Resource:
Disabling browser extensions

http://dsg.tips/ext

Have you ever gotten a notification to do an update and you put it off or ignored it? Because these updates often contain security patches that prevent viruses and malware from compromising your system, don't put it off — install all updates immediately to help keep yourself safe. This doesn't only apply to your operating system or word processor but includes ALL electronic devices you have. People are not very conscious about protecting their mobile devices and their tablets from external threats. You have to protect your phones and tablets both physically and digitally, and the simplest way is keeping them up-to-date.

Many people try and avoid upgrading or updating their software, operating systems, phones, etc., because sometimes things didn't go as smoothly as expected. They use this as a reason to wait until the update bugs have been worked out, and there are no reports of updates going wrong. Although this may reduce the chance of the update or upgrade having glitches, it doesn't mean it is a sure thing. Either way, you should be using proper data backup and synchronization, so if something does go wrong, it should only be a brief inconvenience. It is also important to note that things don't usually go wrong with minor updates — significant upgrade problems usually only happen during a major update to the software. It may be okay to wait a short period of time to do a major upgrade as the purpose of the update is mainly new features, not bug and security fixes.

 **Tip**

Even minor updates should be done immediately — don't make excuses.

One thing to be aware of when updating cell phone software is that most phones use a legacy methodology of rolling out software updates by having them go from the manufacturer to the telecom provider and then finally to the customer. This extra hop in the middle can result in updates taking days, weeks and sometimes months longer than they should to get the update into your hands. Also, in many cases, the telecom provider is inserting their own tracking, apps, and other junk into the software. One of the truly amazing things Apple was able to do with the iPhone was put an end to this absurd practice. iPhone updates go directly from Apple to the customer. If you use Android, Blackberry, Windows, or another cell phone, you should be aware that your automatic update might be waiting for your telecom provider and leaving you exposed.

Jailbreaking

A quick note on jailbreaking: don't do it. Jailbreaking is when you modify the software on your device in a way that was not intended so that you can circumvent or use the device in new ways. In July 2015, an Italian company called Hacking Team, a company that wrote malware and spy software that it sold to governments around the world, was, ironically, hacked. The hackers leaked an enormous amount of data including the exploits and software sold by Hacking Team. It turned out the only platform they couldn't infect was the iPhone, with the exception of jail-broken iPhones, in which case they could take full control of it like they could on all the other cell phones, desktops, etc.

Jailbreaking can also stop your update feature from working, which means you will not get critical security patches and bug fixes.

Proper security & authentication

Ensure that your device is properly secured. The first and easiest step for this is having a password. Your phone needs to have a password or pin code! It's unacceptable not to have a password on your phone. Yes, it is inconvenient. But a phone without a password is incredibly easy to take complete control of it. Not to mention that all of your data on your phone including pictures, phone numbers, addresses, apps, etc. will be accessible by a hacker or thief. I'm sure you have some apps that don't require a password to open up either, which might be abused by someone who takes your phone.

I also recommend you put a password on every single one of your devices — every single one. If the device never leaves your home, then you may think, what for? In the event that the device is stolen, there is no protection on your data or from them using the device. Maybe it's just a kid's laptop or tablet — what do they really need a password for? They don't have anything important on it. Maybe, maybe not. The device is connected to your wireless network, which is shared with your other computers. It is probably connected to your cloud accounts. Do you want to have any chance of recovering the device? The chances are that the device will leave home at some point. This may be a good opportunity to start teaching your kids best security practices.

If you are still not inclined to secure these devices, don't forget that they have cameras and microphones on them. There have been numerous cases of hackers using the cameras on laptops and wireless baby cameras to spy on and even blackmail people. The thought that someone could be watching or listening to a private household through a computer, phone, or tablet is creepy and criminally intrusive, to say the least — and it happens!

You should check if your device supports encryption — encryption is only useful if you have a password. Most computers and mobile devices support encryption these days.

Did you know?

▶ As of 2013, nearly 40% of users did not use a password to secure their phone [43]

Locating and remote erasing

Do you have a contingency plan in place if one of your devices is lost or compromised? Better to know you are properly set up to handle this now than to wait for it to be stolen and realize you didn't enable something you should have. This should include your mobile phones, tablets, laptops, and even your desktop that doesn't leave your house — what if someone breaks in and steals it while you are away on vacation?

Apple's Find My Phone tool suite is an excellent solution to this problem. Take the time and log into Find My Phone to make sure that all your devices are viewable and you can pinpoint the location on all of them. In an emergency where your device has been lost or stolen, you can use that tool to recover the device. It also allows you to set off an alarm, wipe the device of all data, display a message on the screen, and view its location on a map.

Windows phones have a Find My Phone feature, as do Android phones with Android Device Finder. Apple's Find My Phone is especially nice since it can also control and track your laptop or desktop computer. If you are using a Microsoft Windows laptop or desktop, you will need to use a third-party solution. For a detailed tutorial of setting up tracking on your Apple, Android, or Microsoft devices, see here:

Resource: Find my phone

`http://dsg.tips/phone`

When talking about a preparedness plan, you should also consider not only if it is stolen, but what if it becomes infected with a virus, crashes, is destroyed in a home fire, or someone spills a glass of water on it. Your data backup and recovery are going to be critical in this scenario. You don't want to try and recover your data from a failed hard drive — it will be very costly and may have lackluster results. Make sure you are using a proper data backup solution and using it diligently.

Don't plug it in!

Everyone has had the problem of their cell phone battery dying or getting too low. Especially if they're at a big event, concert, conference, sporting event or at the airport. What do you do when your battery is low and there is a sign that says free phone charger? You plug your phone in without a second thought. With advances in technology, we now use the same port on our phones to charge as we do for data. When you plug your phone into what appears to be a charging cable that goes inside some kiosk, you may not know about a little computer back there which takes full control of your phone and inserts a virus on it, while charging your phone for free of course. Plugging anything into your devices can open your device up to a completely new attack vector. There were some clever hackers that pulled this trick on people at a security conference and were quite successful.[44]

I recommend you always use your own charger and plug it directly into the AC outlet. Some of the new laptops are using this technology of combining the data and charging port on your computer — you should be aware of this before plugging in willy-nilly.

Also, keep in mind that anything you plug into your computers or phones could have unintended consequences. It has been rumored that highly secured facilities have been breached by someone simply plugging an unknown USB stick into their computer. Maybe they found it in their home driveway, the office parking lot, or simply on or near their desk. Although your intentions may be that of a good Samaritan, and you simply want to see if you can determine whom it belongs to so you can return it, you could be letting a virus loose on your computer and network. This is exactly what happened earlier in the book when Ghost, the social engineering hacker, convinced secretary Amanda, to help print his resume from his USB stick. Don't plug unknown things into your computer. You wouldn't risk eating an unfamiliar berry or mushroom – don't let your devices take the same risk.

Remember

Plugging or inserting anything into your one of your devices could pose a security risk of some sort.

Leaving your device unattended with anyone who could plug something into your device is also a risk you should think about. For example, if airport security takes your phone or laptop to a private room in another country, they could have potentially plugged something into it which may have given them access or future access to your phone and data. We'll talk more about traveling with digital devices later.

Virus scan

The newest generation of viruses are much more sophisticated than those of only two or three years ago— they spread more intelligently and are constantly finding new ways to take advantage of us.

The unfortunate reality is that viruses, malware, trojans, worms, and other types of computer infections are still quite common. Some programs pretend to be a virus scanner or remover and tell you to pay for their premium version to get the virus removed — in return, they might steal your credit card number. Others will encrypt your data and then make you pay a ransom to regain access to it, know as ransomware. This type of virus infected several police departments in 2013 after an employee opened a malicious email attachment. Some will infect your browser and Internet browsing experience, stealing credentials or bombarding you with ads and redirecting you to websites you weren't trying to go to. Some viruses sit dormant and wait until hackers want to use your computer and Internet connection to DDoS a website (bombard a website with so much fake traffic that it disrupts their service). Some infections are used to get deeper into a network you may have access to, like your work, healthcare if you are a doctor, or your university network if you are an educator. We now have to assume these same types of viruses are trying to sneak their way into our tablets and mobile devices.

I recommend that you run a virus scan tool, especially if you are running Windows. Many of the best scanners out there also include browser plugins that can protect you from threats on the web, including ones that try to exploit your browser or another browser plugin. Even a trusted website can end up with some bad code injected on a few pages by skilled hackers. It is scary to think you can get infected simply by visiting a website. Yes, a virus scanner may slow down your computer a little bit and cost a little bit of money, but it is an additional layer of security to help protect you. If you have kids, especially teenagers, you may find that they tend to be less aware of security issues on the Internet and will be enticed to download and open things without realizing they are packed with a virus.

I also recommend that you completely reformat your computer every year or two. Not only does this help clean out the junk and possibly speed things up, but it can help ensure any lurking virus you may have gotten is wiped out. This may seem like a lot of work, but by taking a few simple steps up front, you can make this much easier. Keep a list of all the software you use and the serial or key numbers (storing this as an encrypted list, of course, and not storing it in the cloud unencrypted). Then, ensure all of your documents are properly backed up — this habit should already be in place. You can then do a reinstall of your operating system, sync from your backup, and install your list of programs from that list. The first time you may find a few things you would change in the future. If you have a more complicated setup on your computer, as many developers would have, I highly recommend you look into using VM's (Virtual Machines) to keep those environments isolated and simply put them into your backup strategy. Many people have probably never formatted their computer, and it may be a daunting prospect. Here are some tutorials that can help you. If the inconvenience of this is too much, consider doing it at an interval that you are comfortable with.

If you have kids, I highly recommend you format your computer more often. They don't understand the consequences of clicking, opening, and installing things on the computer and they tend to wander the Internet, as their curiosity takes them, often to questionable websites. They also fall victim to bait appearing as things that interest them, for example "game cheats" or tips. If you share your computer with your kid, you may want to use a VM, Virtual Machine, so that they are operating in an isolated environment and less likely to infect your computer. A bonus to using this method is you can create a snapshot after you get them all setup and can regularly (monthly or quarterly) reset their virtual computer back to a fresh state with everything installed with just the click of a button. This is also covered in the tutorials below.

Resource: Format your devices

http://dsg.tips/format

Buying & Selling used devices

If you buy a used electronic device, like a computer, tablet, phone, etc., before setting it up, you should format or reinstall the software. This means doing a fresh install of the operating system. I even encourage you to do this with devices like wireless routers. The reason I recommend this is because you don't want unexpected malware lurking on your newly purchased device. It could be something installed on it before it was sold or it could be something that infected their device without the seller even knowing. Chances are the person you bought from probably wasn't as security-conscious or as safe as you. Even though you may be very excited to start using your new device, take the time and do a fresh software install to ensure your safety.

When selling a device, not only should you do a fresh install of the operating system, but you should also securely wipe the device, i.e., remove all traces of your data.

When selling any device that contains a memory card, do not sell the memory card with the device. Remove it before selling so you can securely dispose of it — don't take a chance that deleted data might be recoverable. Also, if the device has a removable SIM card (most cell phones do, and sometimes tablets and laptops will as well), also remove it for safe disposal.

Wireless cameras

Wireless cameras have become risky to use. Many people set them up incorrectly or fail to do a thorough setup of their camera. This results in the camera using the default password — hackers then scan the Internet looking for these cameras and try the default and common passwords. There are websites that list thousands of cameras like this. These cameras are not just in public areas or inside of businesses, but many are inside and outside of private homes.

Did you know?

▶ Thousands of home security cameras are connected to the Internet without password protection, allowing anyone to view what they record.

▶ There are tens of thousands more cameras connected to the Internet with the default password, easily accessible to anyone.

Computerworld reported in early 2015 that a nanny, Ashley Stanley, heard a man's voice saying "What a beautiful baby" coming from the wireless baby monitor camera stationed near her one-year-old, Samantha. Spooked and suspecting someone was playing a prank on her, Ashley switched off the camera and began calling around. It wasn't a joke: the parents had never changed the camera's password from its default setting, and a man had easily hijacked the device to broadcast his own voice into the baby's room. This followed reports from the previous two years, also concerning wireless baby monitor cameras, but with less innocuous perpetrators: some of them had sounded unhinged, hurling expletives at the babies and parents and frightening the entire household. Although, as Ashley later told reporters, her own greatest fear was not of the pranksters with nothing interesting to say, but of the knowledge that there might be silent watchers out there, quietly stalking a child or a family.[45]

To understand the severity of this issue, you may want to check out these cameras yourself. Note, these sites are trying to raise awareness, and they do filter out many of the more explicit or dangerous cameras.

Resource: Insecure cameras

http://dsg.tips/opencam

To make things even riskier, security researchers have found that wireless (and wired) cameras (ironically labeled as security cameras by some retailers) are vulnerable and able to be hacked quite easily. Even trusted names and expensive, high-end cameras are vulnerable to these easy hacks.[46]

So what camera should you select, and what should you look for? I am keeping an updated list of ones I recommend here:

Resource:
Security camera recommendations

http://dsg.tips/cam

Even the cameras on laptop and desktop screens can be compromised. There was a proof of concept done where a team of testers were actually able to access the camera on an Apple laptop without causing the green, active light, to turn on. Because of this, it is becoming common practice for people to put a piece of tape over the camera unless they are using it. I do this, and you might want to consider it as well, especially if you don't often use the camera.

Photo Metadata (GPS)

Many people don't realize that when they take a photo on their phone, it attaches metadata to that image. Metadata includes information like what time the photo taken and sometimes the actual GPS positioning of where the photo was taken. This means there is a record of the exact position you were standing in when you took the photo attached to it. Because it is attached to the photo as metadata, you don't see it when you look at the photo. Now, having GPS coordinates attached to your photos can be awesome. It can be used to give you great ways to view where you've been and what pictures you took on what vacations. However, it can also mean that you're exposing sensitive information you may not have wanted to. For example, maybe you're taking a selfie to send to a prospective date you've met online, but you're not ready for them to know where you live. By sending them that selfie with GPS information, you may be giving them the exact position of your home.

In April 2012, the FBI caught Texas hacker Higinio Ochoa on the basis of photo metadata. They were pursuing a hacking group called CabinCr3w, who were responsible for leaking email addresses and confidential information from Goldman Sachs executives in September 2011. They specifically sought an individual who sometimes posted under Anonw0rmer and other times as w0rmer. Higinio's name was associated with the w0rmer alias on a handful of online posts, and then, after a particularly harmful law enforcement agency hack, a photo was posted of a woman in a low-cut top – face out of frame – with a triumphant message propped up just below her breasts, signed "w0rmer." The photo had GPS metadata that corresponded to Higinio's girlfriend's home. He was arrested at gunpoint, interrogated, and charged by the FBI. He took a plea deal and was sentenced to 27 months in prison. The judge also issued him with a total ban from the internet.[47]

Did you know?

▶ In 2007, a new fleet of helicopters arrived at a US aviation unit in Iraq. Some soldiers took pictures and uploaded them to the Internet, giving the enemy the exact location of the helicopters inside the compound. A mortar attack struck shortly afterward, destroying four of the AH-64 Apaches.[48]

Be aware of this happening, and that you could be revealing information you didn't want to. You can disable this automatic position tagging functionality inside your phone settings. I recommend you do that in some scenarios, especially on your kids' phones. It can be daunting to think of valuable, expensive hardware being compromised and

to realize how easily your devices could be hacked. By raising your awareness and taking the steps suggested in this
chapter, you should keep your vulnerability to a minimum.

TWELVE

WHITE HAT HACKERS

Surprise, you're dead!

A SECURITY researcher named Chris Rock revealed his research at the 2015 DEFCON hacking conference on how easy it is to make someone legally dead. He didn't stop there: he also showed how easy it is to create a new identity, a legitimate registered virtual baby with a social security number and all.

It turns out it is very easy to make someone legally dead. Obviously, it is VERY ILLEGAL to do this and as such, don't try it. So, how did he do it? In the US, we use a web service called the Electronic Death Registration System (EDRS). To use this service, a doctor must register using their name, license number, and address. It turns out that all that information is public information and in many states you can simply look that information up or validate it online. Since most general practitioners don't register, it is easy to find a doctor who hasn't previously registered.

However, to declare someone dead and get a death certificate, you also need a funeral director. Turns out, though, you don't need anything special to become a funeral director — you simply file an application and wait for approval. That is pretty much all there is to it. There are many reasons someone might try and digitally kill someone off, and all of them are malicious. In some cases, people might want to kill themselves off to collect their life insurance policy and then disappear to another country.

You might think that someone filing you as legally dead might be a minor inconvenience, but it can actually be a major problem. One man from Ohio disappeared one day and went to work elsewhere in the country without telling anyone. He stayed unplugged and out of touch. After a few years, his ex-wife requested he be declared dead so she could apply for Social Security benefits for their two daughters. She wasn't trying to be malicious or work the system: she legitimately thought he was dead. A few years later the man resurfaced while trying to apply for a driver's license. However, you can't get a license if you are legally dead, so he went to court. The judge denied his request to reverse his death, as Ohio law does not allow a declaration of death to be reversed after three years have passed.

Apparently the law, as well as the security protocols that protect these systems, have not caught up with recent technology and security advancements. It is even easier to create a new virtual person by using the Electronic Birth Registration (EBR) system. Not only do you not need a funeral director, but you can use a midwife or a doctor, both of which are listed in public records.

There is nothing you can do to protect yourself from this, which is what makes it so scary. Now that this information is so well-known, we hope to see the industry make significant improvements to the security of these systems. As the general public, all we can do is stand behind the security researchers, help file complaints with these organizations, and reach out to Congressmen and Senators to elicit their help in fixing these issues. As part of an initiative to help, I have put together resources to make it as easy as possible to make your voice heard and motivate governments and related organizations to make changes and take security seriously.

Resource: Support security research

`http://dsg.tips/showsupport`

Hacking cars and garages

With the introduction of more electronic and connected devices, there are new opportunities for those devices to be exploited or hacked. A scary new example of this as of 2015 is the hacking of cars. At the 2015 DEFCON, the annual hacker and security researcher conference, many security issues with vehicles and security systems came to light. Samy Kamkar, a security researcher, created a device that for $30 can open most fixed-code garage door openers in under 10 seconds. He also created a device that could open rolling-code garage doors and rolling-code car lock key fobs by jamming the signal when you try to use them and capturing your key fob transmission for later use.

Remember

Although car manufacturers are quickly trying to find ways to improve the security of these remote key fobs, many products, like your garage door opener, will never see a software update, making them vulnerable forever (or until you replace them).

These attacks against everyday technologies, unfortunately, get much scarier. At the 2015 DEFCON conference, I also saw examples of vehicle entertainment and control systems being hacked. In one example, hackers found vulnerabilities in the Tesla Model S that allowed them to turn the vehicle on and off. However, the Tesla Model S was by most standards very secure, and hacking into it would require prolonged physical access to the inside of the car. Even better, Tesla patched the vulnerabilities and sent an update to all of the existing vehicles within a week. This is quite incredible, especially when you compare it to the next example, the hacked Jeep.

Security researchers were able to take remote control of a Jeep and shut the vehicle off while it was traveling 70 mph on the freeway. Jeep issued a recall for 1.4 million vehicles from 2013 and newer with the Chrysler Uconnect system. Unlike Tesla, where every car could be fixed in a matter of days, it will take months if not years for all the affected Jeeps to be updated and will cost Chrysler millions of dollars.

Yet another hack against vehicles was an attack against vehicles with OnStar. If you use the OnStar app within the vicinity of a hacker with the right equipment, you'll find the hacker can then monitor your position, unlock your car, and start or stop the vehicle indefinitely. Luckily the issue was mostly with the OnStar app on mobile phones, and OnStar issued an update to patch this vulnerability.

Security researchers like the ones at DEFCON identify these types of bugs and report them to the manufacturers to get them fixed. They then write articles, do presentations and talks about their findings, explain how they found them and how to protect against them. When this happens, the bugs get fixed, and hopefully, those bugs fixes are able to reach your device in a reasonable amount of time. However, hackers and malicious organizations don't publicly release their findings. They also don't tell the manufacturer about the bug. Instead, they use their knowledge maliciously as long as they possibly can.

Unfortunately, not all companies take kindly to security researchers or "white hat" hackers who poke around and publicly exploit their systems. This has resulted in many professionals who are trying to help protect the public being arrested, charged, jailed, or fined for harmlessly "hacking" or exploiting a company's system. Many companies would rather sweep such issues under the rug than have them publicly released. Sometimes they ignore contact from security researchers altogether – even if the message would only benefit the company and its clients. This culture is changing, though, and many companies have programs where they will pay security researchers for finding and disclosing the bug to them prior to releasing it to the public.

I personally reached out to two healthcare organizations via email asking to be put in contact with someone to discuss a security vulnerability, only to get no response at all.

If you do see news articles about security researchers being arrested, or young, well-intentioned hackers getting into trouble, join the cause and help support them. These security researchers are looking out for your best interests, and they are going up against Goliath-sized companies with large legal teams who are publicly embarrassed – a scary opponent for anyone.

THIRTEEN

DIGITAL REPUTATION SYSTEMS

Banking systems

MANY PEOPLE do not realize that banks use their own reputation system. It doesn't contain a lot of information about your accounts and history with the bank, but it does give insight into where you hold accounts and what the account status is. If you are serious about protecting your identity, you should request this report yearly. This will let you know if someone has opened a bank account in your name. Not all banks will do a credit check when opening an account, so this is another way to catch that fraudulent activity.

Resource: Bank reputation systems

http://dsg.tips/bank

DMV

The DMV also runs their own reputation system about you. Your driving record includes the status of your license, traffic law violations or convictions you may have gotten, DUI or DWI records, and how many points you have on your license. Each state uses points differently, so to see how your state operates or to acquire your DMV driving record, see here:

Resource: DMV driving history

http://dsg.tips/dmv

It is good to check this yearly as it may show signs of someone else using your identity. Additionally, mistakes happen and false information could be on your record. This can result in significantly higher insurance rates. Before you apply for auto insurance, you should give your DMV Driving Record and the insurance reputation systems a check — read more about those below. If you have a ticket or point about to drop off or expire, it may be beneficial to wait for that to happen before applying for new insurance.

If you have been a victim of identity theft, it may be worthwhile to check the NHTSA (National Highway Traffic Safety Administration) and the National Driver Register (NDR) to see if your identity may have been used in another state to register for a driver's license. You can do so by visiting the resource below.

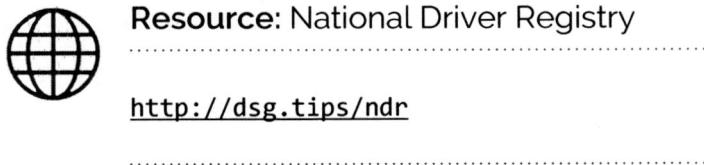

Resource: National Driver Registry

`http://dsg.tips/ndr`

Insurance systems

Insurance companies also use their own reputation system called CLUE (Comprehensive Loss Underwriting Exchange). Again, many people do not know this exists, or, if they do, they hardly ever think to check it. If you have filed an auto insurance claim, then you can be sure they have reported it to their system. This will affect your eligibility and pricing when you apply for auto insurance elsewhere. This is also not limited to auto insurance. Homeowner's insurance companies (including renter's insurance) will also report to CLUE. I recommend you pull your CLUE report yearly to check for any signs of fraud and before you make any changes to your insurance plans.

Remember

It may be to your benefit, as with the DMV driving record, to wait a month or two before changing insurance companies or adjusting your plan — there may be a negative item about to drop off.

Medical Records

Medical records are another digital system that tracks a lot about you. Medical records are not aggregated into some central or government database. This is good and bad. You do have a right to get access to your medical records at any institution you have been to. You may need to pay for copies and mailing. This cost varies by state but is considered to be reasonable.

Most people won't check their medical records for fraud, and you probably don't need to unless you have a reason to be concerned. Someone receiving medical care under your name is still fairly rare. However, there are scenarios where if someone uses your name, information could become merged and incorrect, leading to injury or death. For example, a medication you may be allergic to could get erased from your medical record. Or your blood type could get changed in the computer. If you get a health insurance bill for unknown services, you may want to request your medical records to ensure everything is correct.

Social Security

The Social Security Organization collects information about your yearly income and reports that to the IRS. At times, your social security number could be used by an illegal resident for employment. This will result in all their wages being reported under your social security number. What will happen is that you will file your taxes and declare your income based on your W-2, but then you will get flagged by the IRS for not declaring income from the additional job with W-2 that someone else got under your identity. This can result in an unexpected and nasty tax bill. The Social Security administration's website will allow you to log in and view your earnings once a year to verify the amounts are correct (see http://www.socialsecurity. gov/myaccount/). They will also list the amount of Social Security and Medicare taxes you have paid. Not only is it a good idea to check this yearly to validate your own numbers, but also to ensure no one else is piggybacking on your identity.

The IRS maintains an exhaustive list of examples of real identity theft cases. In August 2015, they reported the conviction of a California man who obtained the personal identifying information of numerous people and filed tax returns in their names. He fraudulently claimed tax credits that landed him with over $250,000 in refunds. After being caught, the man was sentenced to 42 months in prison, three years of supervised release, and a restitution payment of $285,034.[49]

Perhaps scarier, a Georgia woman was sentenced in July 2015 for filing over 180 false tax returns. She had obtained her victims' identifying information via her real job fielding phone calls for a major health insurer.[50]

Vehicle history

Vehicle history and title information feed into another reputation system. However, automotive industry regulation is relatively fragmented, so there is no central authority for all of the data out there about your car. This has led to companies like Carfax becoming popular. Carfax acquires and aggregates public data from dozens of sources and combines them into a trusted report about your vehicle history.

Although there isn't a need to do ongoing monitoring of your car(s) on Carfax, it is something you should check before selling your car. Potential buyers are going to want to see the Carfax report from you or they will buy it themselves. You don't want to be in the middle of selling the car when the potential buyer notices an irregularity on your report. One time my Carfax report had an alert for a modified odometer, claiming I may have removed miles. Turns out, it was just an incorrect mileage entered by someone doing basic maintenance on the car — nothing that couldn't be easily resolved.

 **Tip**

Never buy a used car without getting the Carfax report.

For discounts, and the best information on getting a vehicle history report, check out this resource:

Resource: Carfax

`http://dsg.tips/carfax`

Future systems

When you look at the current state of our reputation systems, the field seems ripe for innovation. Many systems haven't been changed in decades, and as technology has progressed, more information continues to be crammed into old, inflexible systems.

Credit scores and credit bureaus create a flawed dynamic. If you wanted to get the best possible rate on a car loan, with the few clicks of a button you could have your information sent to a dozen loan providers, who would each pull your credit. These 12 hard inquiries will look horrible on your credit report, will significantly drop your score, and will stick with you for the next two years. There is absolutely room for more sophisticated (and humane) advancement in this area of digital record and reputation systems.

Finance and insurance companies are trying new things in this area. For example, new algorithms can look at your social network profiles to build a better risk model or identify red-flag spending habits. It is likely that lenders will want to automatically analyze your bank and credit card transactions to better understand your spending habits before lending to you. We don't know exactly what the next generation of systems will look like, but we can be sure they are coming soon.

Credit reports

Credit reports are one of the most popular digital reputation systems we all use. Because credit scores are so important, the next chapter is entirely devoted to them.

In this chapter, we covered the little-known reputation systems used by the institutions we rely on most: banks, the DMV, insurance companies, and healthcare providers. In the next chapter, we'll deep dive into the most important digital reputation system of them all: your credit report.

FOURTEEN

CREDIT REPORT

Building credit

THIS FIRST part of this section is tailored to people who have no credit card or credit history. Although building credit is a bit beyond the scope of this book, it is a topic I feel is imperative to talk about. Your credit and credit reports are one of the single most important digital reputations you have. We will cover why it's significant, exactly what you need to be doing to be building your credit, and how to protect it.

Did you know?

- A late credit-card payment will stay on your credit report for seven years.[51]
- A hard credit inquiry will stay on your record for 24 months.[52]

Some people may advise you not to get a credit card, especially when you are young because it can get you into a lot of trouble. Your first credit card, probably a student credit card of some sort, is going to have a small limit that may be a lot for you at the time. However, a late payment is a late payment and will significantly disadvantage you. However, not having a credit card means you aren't building any credit. As an 18-year-old, a credit card is the simplest way to start building that credit. When you and your friends go to rent an apartment a couple of years into college, and none of you have any credit history, you better hope that one of your parents or family members will co-sign for you. However, had you used a credit card responsibly for a couple of years, you would be trusted by the landlord and have a respect worthy credit score, and thus no need for a co-signer. You may also need to get a loan, like a car loan, at some point. Someday you might even want to buy a house – sure, that is probably far off in the future, but credit cards can take 5 to 7 years to build a solid history. If you wait, you are wasting an opportunity.

First, you need to use the card responsibly — when getting your first credit card, don't use it as a line of credit. Use it in place of cash and then pay it off at the end of the month. Follow a strict rule that never under any circumstance do you use it to float or loan yourself money. The moment you get into that financial situation, cut the card and figure out how to do it without borrowing money — you'll figure it out. Once you are stable, you can order a replacement card.

Be very protective of people running your credit — each time someone runs your credit, it can lower your score and stay on your credit report for two years. Going to a website and getting approved for a bunch of cards all at once could result in a dozen hits to your credit report, something that should be avoided at all costs.

Only get one credit card to start out. You have no need for more — after college age, you should get a second card from a different provider.

Don't miss a payment under any circumstance — and don't toe the line paying it right before it is due and risk a late payment. If you know for sure you have to pay it late, call the credit card company immediately, explain the situation, and tell them when you will pay. They will usually work with you in these scenarios. If you cannot afford the payment, look for a way to float the money that would not affect your credit report. For example, your bank might have overdraft protection that would allow you to pay your credit card bill before it is late. Overdraw your bank account by a small amount and eat the $20 overdraft charge. Then speak with your bank about getting your account back to positive before they report it to any credit agency. This can buy you an extra couple of weeks, usually. Late payments are mistakes that will stay on your credit for seven years, seven years! It might not be a big deal now, but it might be a big issue for you five years from now.

At least make the minimum payment — however, do not continue to pay only the minimum payment. The interest you are paying is high, and you cost yourself a lot more money. Get it paid off to zero as quickly as possible. To be safe, you can set up your credit card to pay the minimum payment using auto-withdraw to ensure you never miss a payment.

For my credit card recommendations, including the best sign-up bonuses, have a look here:

Resource:
Credit card recommendations

http://dsg.tips/creditcard

If you find yourself in a situation where you need a loan, but no one will approve you due to your lack of credit (or maybe poor credit), then check out these recommended ways to get credit:

Resource: Bad credit loans

http://dsg.tips/badcredit

Take care when considering closing credit cards. If you have 5+ cards, you should probably consider closing some. You may be able to get one of your existing cards to increase your limit and take on that debt if you are carrying any debt. You should also not close all of them, but strive to have two cards from two different companies and keep them open for life, even if you don't use one or only use it for one small recurring charge a month and set it up to use auto-payment. This will keep your credit history building. Also, closing an account will not remove your payment history, including late payments.

Don't open too many lines of credit, especially in a short period of time. Shopping for credit, buying a car, opening a bank account, and getting into an apartment can all get your credit run, and that can make your credit report look like you may be acquiring too much debt too quickly, which is a red flag. Even some electrical and gas companies (and cell phone providers) may run your credit. Be aware and ensure it is worth it.

Even credit checks stay on your report for two years, so always ask anytime you provide your social security number if they will do a credit check. Sometimes banks will do them when opening an account, apartment complexes will do them, anytime you open a line of credit, buy a car or house, finance anything with multiple payments (new cell phone provider, setting up cable or satellite the first time, electric or gas companies, etc.). Be very protective about letting anyone run a credit check. There is a difference between a hard vs. soft inquiry. However, every single time someone tells me it is only a soft inquiry (meaning it won't show on your credit report), it ends up showing up on my credit report as a hard inquiry. Most of the time, the person who is setting up your account won't even know and will have to ask someone else. When opening a bank account with a new bank, my representative had to ask two people and call a third person to find out it was a soft inquiry and would not show up on my report. Sure enough, it showed up as a hard inquiry on my credit report and when I asked them to remove it as that is not what they told me, they agreed but said I'd also have to close my account. Never give out your social security number for your credit report to be run unless you absolutely have to.

Increasing your score

Increasing your buying power is important for many reasons. It shows lenders that you can be trusted with managing a larger line of credit. It also helps increase your credit score by reducing your available funds use percentage. If you have a credit card with a $500 limit, and you spend $375 on it each month and pay it off fully., your credit report would show that you are using 75% of the money available to you. This level of use reflects negatively on you. By spending the same amount but increasing your credit limit to $1,000, you are now only using 37% of your available credit — this is much more ideal. The recommended level is to stay below 30%, and around 10% will give you your ideal positive impact on your credit score.

Remember

It is smart to keep the inquiries to your credit report to an absolute minimum.

Many institutions will allow you to increase your line of credit without a hard inquiry on your credit report. Some credit card companies will let you increase your limit every six months, and will let you double or triple it without question so long as your account is in good standing. Be sure to pay off your account to zero before putting in the request and you should do some searching online to see what other people's experiences are and what they recommend for your specific credit card. There is a lot of discussion on how to push up your credit limit safely. Within three years you can easily increase your buying power from $500 to $10,000. Eventually, you will reach a limit they are not comfortable with depending on what your income is — usually they will provide you a counteroffer if they don't accept your initial request.

If you are going to apply for a line of credit, especially for a house or car loan, ensure your credit use is down to 10% before you do so. Keep in mind that a payment may take 4 to 6 weeks to reflect on all of your credit reports.

Tip

If your credit report shows that your credit use is down to 10%, the additional bump you will get in your credit score could get you a significantly lower interest rate and save you money on a loan or mortgage.

Here is another way to keep your credit use low. You can call your credit card company and find out the date that they report to the credit bureau — for example, it could be the second business day of the following month.

Tip

By simply moving your payment date to a couple of days before their report date or before the closing of the statement, the credit bureau companies will see a significantly lower balance month to month. This means

> your credit score will be consistently higher
> as you are using less of your available credit
> — keeping you at that ideal 10% or less usage.

You should pay your credit cards down as low as possible before applying for a loan or form of credit to get the best possible rate. This means you have to make a payment before the statement closes, then wait until they report the updated account balance. If it is the beginning of a month and you need to apply for credit, you could have to wait 30 to 40 days before your credit report is updated with that new balance. By moving your regular payment schedule, it can afford you the convenience of always showing a low balance so you won't have to plan so far in advance.

Securing your credit

Credit monitoring is paramount to protecting your identity. You are legally entitled to a free copy of your credit report once a year. At the very least you should be taking advantage of the fact you can get it yearly for free.

Credit card fraud can be costly and extremely time-consuming to recover from. For example, CBS reported in 2005 that John Harrison's identity was stolen by a 20-year-old whose buying spree included two cars, two motorcycles, and dozens of department-store purchases over the course of four months. Harrison, he put in upwards of 2000 hours to get his name cleared and secure again. He began by working with the police, who eventually put the repentant thief in prison for three years. Unfortunately, creditors and collections agents continued to pursue Harrison, whose credit score decreased hundreds of points. His last piece of advice to the reporter was that everyone should check their credit report frequently.[53]

Even if you are young and not building credit yet, check it to make sure no one else has been using your identity. I recommend you consider using a credit monitoring service so that you can be alerted of any changes. Unfortunately, these services will run you $5 to $15 per month. If you can't afford this, then stick to your free yearly credit report and simply pay for the service right before you apply for loans. For example, if you are going to buy a new car or house, then I recommend you get credit monitoring for the month leading up to it. This way you can ensure there will be no surprises, and you can find out immediately if someone runs your credit who maybe shouldn't of. If you can afford the monthly cost, then you shouldn't even question paying for it. Being alerted of someone accessing your credit report means you can react and protect yourself before the thief has their chance to do much damage.

A free alternative is to see if you have been impacted by any recent data breaches. If your information has been compromised by an attack on Home Depot, Target, eBay, or any other major organization, they usually provide free credit monitoring to their customers. If a business you frequent has been hacked, ask if they will be providing free credit monitoring.

Another alternative you should consider is requesting a credit freeze — this will block anyone from requesting or taking out a new line of credit against your identity. There are three different credit reporting companies you would have to do this with, and each one will charge you around

$10 to place the freeze. If you are older than 65 or the victim of identity theft, then you may be able to place a freeze for free. When you need to apply for credit or have your credit report run, you can simply request a temporary lift — check the fee's that may apply. If you are fairly sure you won't need to access your credit report for the next year or two, this might be a great option to ensure security.

If you are a parent, you may also want to check into placing a Protected Consumer/Minor lock on your child's credit. This will prevent anyone from messing with their credit until they are 18, when they should begin monitoring or freezing it themselves.

For a list of credit monitoring services I recommend with reviews and discounts, check out my guide here:

 **Resource:**
Credit report monitoring services

http://dsg.tips/credit

Be aware there are three credit bureau services, and ensure you are able to view all three. Usually, a credit inquiry will only show up on one of the reports, and although open lines of credit should show on all three, it is best to be sure by viewing all three.

Tip

If you can afford it, I highly recommend a service like LifeLock. They offer premium protection.

If you check your credit and find anything negative, you should dispute it. You can do so directly with the credit bureau or if it is a late payment, you can speak to the company who issued it and try to find terms where they will remove it from your record. When disputing with the credit bureau, the company that posted the issue has to respond. If they do not respond, it will be removed after 30 days. However, if they respond after the 30-day window, it could be reinstated. It is worth trying to get it off and negotiating with whoever put it on there for a way to get it removed. A better score can save you thousands in interest over the years on future loans or other lines of credit.

Loans

Loans can be a valuable tool for building credit, but they need to be managed correctly. Many people pull out loans to increase their buying power and purchase one or more things they don't want to wait for. People see them as an opportunity to fulfill their impulsive need to have something, but they don't take into account the amount they will pay in interest. Before you take out a loan, you should understand the total amount, including the interest, that you will pay when it is all over with. You might rethink paying all that extra money to have something now instead of waiting until later. There are many calculators online to help you out with this and many great ways to find loans at reliable rates, with good credit or bad. Check out my guide for this here:

Resource: Best loans

`http://dsg.tips/loan`

If you are interested in some of the newer investment technologies and platforms, I have put together some recommendations online.

Resource:
Investment site recommendations

`http://dsg.tips/invest`

A much better use for a loan is perhaps consolidating your debt. Consolidating can be beneficial as you may be able to score a much lower interest rate. Not to mention, it is significantly easier to manage. Maybe you already have an existing loan of some sort (other than auto or mortgage): is there a way to make payments that will help increase your credit faster? It is hard to know for sure because the way the credit scores are calculated is not publicly disclosed by the credit bureaus. Based on my own experimentation, I would recommend the following:

Pay slightly over the minimum. If your minimum is $50, then I'd pay $75. Even if I could pay $100, I'd stick with $75 and save that extra money — not only does this increase my liquid cash in the event of an emergency, but you can use it to do a larger payoff payment further down the road. Once you have enough money saved up to pay off the loan (and some safety cash), a large final payment where you pay off your loan early can provide you with a nice bump to your score. You will pay more in interest doing this method so you will have to calculate that into your decision. Always ask about prepayment penalties before planning to use this strategy. Ideally, you should never get a loan with prepayment or early payoff penalties.

As with credit cards, never miss or make a late payment on a loan. This will significantly hurt your credit. If you get into a situation where you cannot pay, call your loan provider immediately and discuss with them your plan and options to prevent a late payment. Calling proactively shows responsibility and will increase their cooperation in resolving the issue with a mutually beneficial solution.

In this chapter, we've covered the essentials of establishing and building strong credit. In the next, we'll pursue the credit concept in more depth, starting with one of the most common hacks of all: credit card fraud.

FIFTEEN

DIGITAL MONEY

Credit card fraud

REDIT CARD fraud is the most prevalent type of digital theft and the one most likely to affect you. It isn't so much a matter of if your credit card number will be stolen during your lifetime, but rather a matter of when and how many times. With proper preparation, credit card theft will be more of an inconvenience than a financial and psychological catastrophe.

This type of fraud is so common that nearly everyone has a story. One of the most memorable I've heard is that of Harrun Majeed, a Navy veteran who realized he'd misplaced his credit card at the grocery store cash register. He called the credit card company right away, only to be informed that there was already a fresh charge on the card: $40 had been spent at a nearby pizzeria. Clearly, Harrun had dropped his card on the way to the store, and an impulsive pizza-hungry person had scooped it up. Harrun called the police, who were able to immediately drive over to the pizzeria to ask around. What they found surprised everyone: the culprit was still there, holding Harrun's card and waiting for his pizza to come out of the oven. He was no teenager or down-on-his-luck scrounger, but a dentist with a personal net worth of over $3 million, plus $250 in ready cash in his wallet. For reasons known only to himself, he had decided to defraud a stranger in order to get his pizza, even though he could easily afford it himself.[54]

One security technique that's immediately effective is setting up alerts on transactions over a certain value. Many credit cards and banks have a feature that, when selected, will send a text message directly to your phone if anything over a certain amount is charged. This is a quick way to identify and stop a credit card thief before they have a chance to do more damage. Even better, some credit card companies like American Express have a mobile app that will notify you of all transactions.

Credit card skimming

Credit card numbers are stolen through a number of methods, both physical and virtual. Physically, they can be stolen a few different ways: by credit card skimmers, hidden cameras and NFC readers.

Skimmers

Skimmers are devices that will try to capture your credit card information, and possibly your PIN number when you are using the machine. Sometimes, these look like a face plate that is placed on top of the device — these are designed to blend in with the card reader. Skimmers can also be attached to the electronic wiring inside the device. Unfortunately, it is much harder to see any visual indicator of this. You may notice some machines, like gas pumps, actually have a special piece of security tape on the door that opens to the credit card slot compartment. If that tape is broken, you may want to rethink putting your credit card into that machine. For extensive, up-to-date examples, check out this resource:

Resource:
Skimmer examples and techniques

`http://dsg.tips/skimmer`

If something is visibly attached, bulky, or loose on any credit card machine, you should take that as a red flag. Funny-looking boxes attached with a hole in them, for example, present an obvious red flag. Unfortunately, the technology has improved to the point that it is sometimes nearly impossible to detect.

Hidden Cameras

Increasingly, thieves use pinhole-sized cameras and mount them above the ATM or credit card machine to capture the number and the PIN. One way to reduce your risk is to simply use the ATM inside the branch. Although more in-convenient, it is a lot safer. I personally avoid using ATM's unless I absolutely need to. The ATM attached to the outside of the bank is probably safer than a standalone ATM in a store, which is probably safer than a stand-alone ATM box you see at a fair or in a bar.

Fake ATM

Ever see those standalone ATM boxes? You might be surprised to learn that they may not be legitimate – despite being located in a busy area. It might just be stealing your details when you try to use it. Use extra caution when you see standalone ATM's, especially if they are outdoors.

NFC

If your credit can be swiped by simply waving it in front of the credit card machine instead of swiping it, then it uses NFC technology (near-field communications — think radio waves). Criminals have come up with small devices that can steal your credit card number from inside your wallet just by standing next to you. You can protect yourself with an RFID blocking sleeve or wallet. This has become significantly less of an issue with fewer cards having RFID and the industry moving towards chip-and-PIN. However, many cards still support the older more insecure methods.

 **Resource:** RFID credit card protector

http://dsg.tips/rfid

Credit card imprints

Be alert when handing your credit card over to someone else for processing. If they swipe your card in more than one device, you should be suspicious. Also, watch for any situation where the store might take a carbon copy of your credit card — this is where they use the old-school manual machine that slides over the entire card. Or they put your card under the receipt and rub back and forth until the number is visible on their receipt. If they photocopy or manually write down your credit card number, these are not acceptable practices of handling credit cards. These are all red flags and in the event one appears, you need to raise the issue. Even if they aren't going to steal your credit card, they are making it easy for someone to steal it from them, or increasing the possibility that they could lose it.

I once had a pizza delivery where they imprinted my credit card by rubbing my credit card on the driver's copy of the receipt. Not only could he steal my credit card number or sell it, but he could also easily lose it. And who knows what happens to it after it gets back to the pizza place? How long do they keep that?! I emailed the pizza place's ownership — a week later I got a reply from the owner where he apologized and explained why they were doing it and how they were going to change their process to be more proper. Awesome, I thought — making a difference! Then several weeks later I got another email from the owner. It was an email talking about how candidate XYZ had passed the background check and included other personal information about this potential new employee of theirs. While looking at the email, I noticed the original email to the owner was from another employee named Roy. I assume the owner was replying and using the wrong auto-completed address, thus sending to me instead of his store manager. This happened a couple more times... needless to say, this pizza place was not very security-conscious. This just shows how even well-intentioned people can leak your information.

 **Tip**

Keep in mind that even while standing in line, people often hold their credit card in their hand by their side. It is very easy for someone next to or behind you to take a picture with their smartphone and steal your card information.

EMV (Chip-and-PIN)

Credit card technology is slowly catching up in the U.S., and in 2015 we are finally seeing a mandatory rollout of the EMV technology, also known as Chip-and-PIN.

If your credit card has the EMV chip, then you should pay by inserting your card, so it uses the chip instead of swiping it like you normally do. This will help protect your credit card number from being stolen. However, it may be a while before we discontinue use of the older magnetic strip. EMV does not mitigate the risk when trying to pay for something online and you type in your credit card number.

Other technologies like Apple Pay mitigate risk by preventing your true card number from being released when you make a financial transaction, similar to EMV. These are technologies you should be using.

Debit vs. Credit

One of the biggest mistakes that consumers make is using their debit card to pay for things. By this, I mean that you are selecting "debit" and using your PIN number. You will notice that your debit card probably carries the Visa or MasterCard logo on it; this means that you can also run your same debit card as a credit card. There are a couple of reasons you should select "credit" and never use your PIN number (unless at an ATM) when using your debit card.

First, when you run your card as credit you are essentially spending the bank's money, and the bank is putting a hold on your money until the transaction clears. When you run it as debit, you are essentially using a check and withdrawing that money directly from your account. This is important in the event your credit card is stolen, and you have to file a dispute to get your money back. You can get your money back significantly faster if you run it as credit than if you ran it as debit. Visa and MasterCard offer fraud protection, and because the money wasn't withdrawn from your account immediately, the bank can issue you a refund very quickly. However, if you use debit, then your dispute could take significantly longer to resolve. There is no good reason to open yourself to such a liability and headache.

Second, if you run the card as debit and use your PIN number, you are using the same PIN number that you use when inserting that card into an ATM. This means that if someone steals your card information and the PIN number, they can now go to an ATM and withdraw money directly out of your account. If this happens, you won't be getting your money back very quickly, if at all. If this happens to you, you need to report it immediately. If you report within two days of discovering, you may only be liable for $50, but by waiting a third day you may be liable for up to $500 of the missing money. Waiting more than 60 days after that month's statement could result in you not being able to get any of your money back. This is why it is important to check your account regularly. Don't open yourself up to this risk — always run your card as credit. By running it as credit you will have reduced liability but will still need to report it within 60 days of the statement which had the fraudulent charges.

Finally, running your card as credit is usually faster. This is especially true if the transaction is small, say, under $25, where you may not even be required to sign.

Checks and money orders

Checks

I don't recommend that you use a personal check, at any time, for any reason. Thinking back, I've only used a personal check maybe two times in my entire life. In reality, I probably didn't even need to use it those two times. There are occasions where you may need a voided check, but really they just need the account number and the routing number on the check. You can easily get those off of your bank statements. If you do electronic statements, you can view those numbers online through your digital statements. Checks are slow to write, slow to process, create additional bank balancing overhead, and are susceptible to a lot of fraud. If you are using them, then it may be time to reconsider why. You should also not accept personal checks when selling things. Also, do not give a personal check to someone you don't know — you are essentially giving them your bank routing and account number.

If you must use a check to pay for something, like rent, where a landlord may not accept electronic payments, consider using your banks bill pay feature. They will withdraw the money from your account and send a cashier's check on your behalf.

Money Order vs. Cashier's checks

Money orders can be bought at many institutions including supermarkets, liquor stores, etc. The money is paid up front so they are guaranteed and they are usually limited to smaller amounts, under $1,000. If you need a larger amount than that, then you should get a cashier's check. Cashier's checks are issued by banks and are also paid upfront. It is generally safe to accept money orders and cashier's checks from other people — it is preferable over a personal check.

Isolate and diversify your money

Isolating, diversifying or compartmentalizing your digital money is smart. As people acquire more money and assets, keeping them in one place puts them at much greater risk of being completely wiped out by fraud. Generally speaking, you should never keep more than what the FDIC will insure you for, usually $250,000. The banks probably won't alert you that you have deposited more than what is insured or that you shouldn't keep all of your money in your one account with them — it is in their best interest to have as much money as you will keep with them.

Let's say you have $20,000 in your bank account. I recommend you have a separate bank account with a separate institution and that you move money over there as your liquid savings. This secondary account should be treated like a cold account — one where you never use the ATM card for it, you never even carry the ATM card with you, and you never use checks for it. Ideally, I'd recommend that you don't even link the account to your normal bank account. The best way to move money in and out of that account would be small cash deposits or, even better, a cashier's check. If that is too inconvenient for you, then I recommend you link your secondary account to pull money from your primary account. Since you log into your primary account more often, it is more likely to get hacked, and if they hack into it, you don't want them seeing your secondary bank account listed where they can then initiate a transfer and pull the money from your secondary into your primary. But by linking the opposite way, if someone does access your secondary, they could pull the remainder of your money from your primary — your only additional security is that you access that account less often and from more secure environments (hopefully).

Remember

Having a secondary account is important in the event you do get struck by fraud. With

the primary account frozen, you can switch
everything to your secondary account while
the investigation is being processed.

You can also use this same technique by moving money
from your checking to your savings account within one institution. This will not protect you if your entire account
is compromised, but it will limit the amount someone can
steal if they steal your debit card and PIN or simply try to
cash out your bank account. Don't leave a majority of your
money in one account, especially if there is a debit card tied
to it. Move extra money to your savings account.

If you have a lot of money, you should probably diver-
sify further into other less liquid investments, but that is
beyond the scope of this book.

Do not wire money

Do not wire money to someone, ever! It is like sending cash,
and you're not going to get it back in the event of fraud.
There is no need for you to be doing this and many people
fall for scams that use this method. We have all heard of the
"Nigerian prince" scams and made fun of them, but the fact
is they wouldn't still exist if they didn't work. These types of
scams often target senior citizens and result in them sending money overseas. If you do the same, you will never see
that money again.

Wire fraud, like any cyber crime, can occur on a small
scale but most often hits the headlines when a CEO or corporation is affected. In August 2015, the security news and

investigation site Krebs on Security reported that networking firm Ubiquiti Networks Inc. had $46.7 million stolen from their accounts via fraudulent wire transfers. Cyber thieves gained access to high-ranking employees' email accounts, either by phishing or emailing employees from a look-alike domain name. That is a domain name one or two letters off from the target company's true domain name (for example, if the target company's domain was "example.com" the thieves might register "example.com" or "example.co"). They were seamlessly able to wire the funds, or rather instruct that the wire should be executed. When the report was published, a mere $8.1 million of the stolen funds had been recovered.[55]

Foreign lotteries

Don't play any form of foreign lottery. Federal law makes it illegal for you to do so. Additionally, there are many scams around getting people to play foreign lotteries, most of which are completely fake. Some of these go so far as to actually send you a legitimate-looking check, sometimes even before you play. Cashing that check can possibly expose your account information to the criminals and the check will most definitely bounce, but you won't find out until weeks later after you have spent the money.

Choosing and protecting PIN numbers

What does a good PIN number look like? We talked about what a good password looks like, and a PIN number operates under many of the same rules. There are interesting studies that show most common PINs, and as you would expect 1234, 1111, and 2580 (straight down the number pad) are extremely common PINs. If you think you're being clever, you're probably not. Many people will spell part of their name or their birthday, relative's birthday, or something like that. Just like with passwords, don't do these things. I would simply roll a dice four or five times to get your new PIN number. Make it as long as they will allow it to be.

That's your new PIN number, and after a short while using it, it will be committed to memory, and you won't forget it. Most people never change their PIN numbers, and I have never heard of banks recommending you change. But from a commonsense security standpoint, you should probably change them from time to time — do you even remember the last time you changed yours? Commit to doing so once a year.

You probably also don't want the same PIN number across all of your accounts. You could pick one 3-digit number, let's say 942, and then the fourth number could be based on some number on your card, like the first number of the second to last group. This way you have unique PIN numbers for all your cards but have an easy way to remember what it is. Don't use any of the first numbers if you use this method; try using numbers from the second half of the card. And don't use more than one digit from the card.

Since ATM skimmers sometimes use small cameras to record the PIN number as you enter it, I also think about how I can make my PIN harder to read from prying eyes and cameras. When typing my PIN number, I always put all three fingers on the PIN pad right on the row above the middle. I think of it as the default hand setup for a PIN pad.

After you practice your PIN using this method, you can then add fake movements to your fingers. It is much harder to tell which of the numbers you pushed when you have your finger over three keys than it is if you take one highly exposed finger and touch the keypad. If you find this too complicated and are going to stick to your index finger-only method, a.k.a. the PIN number revealer, then try softly tapping a number that is not in your password. Not enough to push the number, but just enough to make it harder to decipher by the camera. Since most use audio tones, this may not work to fool someone standing next to you.

Alternatively, use your second hand to fully cover the hand typing the PIN number. If you feel weird about the impression you are giving by covering the PIN pad, try just positioning your body to block the view. This won't do much for protecting from cameras above, however. Nonetheless, being more aware when entering your credentials is a good start.

Next time you are in line paying for something, take a look to see if the person in front of you is paying with debit and watch how publicly they type their PIN. Don't be a creeper about it, just casually glance and you will see how easy it would be for a thief to take advantage of you. (And if you see a friend using debit, maybe tell them about the Digital Survival Guide and how it could help them stop that and other dangerous habits.)

When choosing a PIN number, keep in mind that most machines and terminals beep. You can usually tell when someone uses the same number twice as they push it really fast a second time before moving onto the next number. When typing your PIN, try to press the buttons with even spaces in between to hide this.

Avoiding Fees

You should understand your bank account and credit card monthly requirements and when you could face fees. Part of the reason for checking your account regularly is to catch any fees early on. Some bank accounts, for example, will waive a monthly fee if you use direct deposit, keep a specific balance, or transfer money back and forth between your checking and savings accounts.

Keep in mind that credit unions and banks may have very different fees and requirements. When selecting a banking institution, be sure to fully understand their benefits and fees. What is best for most people may not be what is best for you, based on your savings and bank usage.

When your bank activity does reveal a random fee, call your bank and question it immediately. Explain to them that you were not aware of any requirement that resulted in the fee and how you want to prevent that from happening again in the future. Usually, they will be lenient and refund you the fee. Some institutions may also have accounts for students or senior citizens that could work to your advantage.

Some credit and charge cards have a yearly membership fee. First-time credit card or charge card users probably want to avoid these types of cards. However, as you become financially stable, some of these programs are worth their value if you use the benefits. Usually, the best benefits are for travelers. If you have one of these cards and are not entirely happy with the benefits, or they made changes you do not like, then call them and express your unhappiness. You can often get them to refund your yearly fee, especially if you are active with the card. It is more important to them that you continue to use the card.

Merchant surcharges

You may have encountered that at some locations, there is an extra fee to use a credit card. Some states have passed a law banning this type of surcharge. There are eleven states that have laws prohibiting merchants from charging consumers with surcharges on credit card transactions: California, Colorado, Connecticut, Florida, Kansas, Maine, Massachusetts, Minnesota, New York, Oklahoma and Texas.[56]

Some states also have laws that allow merchants to offer a discount for cash customers as long as it applies to all customers. None of them do this, though, except for gas stations where a separate cash price is listed. Even if they can't charge you a surcharge in your state, they can enforce a minimum transaction size (i.e. $10 minimum) and refuse to accept your credit card if your order does not meet that minimum. Merchants will usually allow you to use your debit card without paying a fee even on small transactions, but this would require you to disclose your PIN number.

Digital Wallets

PayPal was the first major digital wallet on the Internet. After it came Google Wallet, and now the more recent, phone-optimized payment platforms, Apple Pay and Android Pay. The concept behind all of these is simple: add multiple payment methods to the digital wallet, and then when you pay, the money is sent from the digital wallet, and your payment information (like your credit card number or bank routing information) does not have to be given to the merchant. This will limit your exposure to hackers stealing your credit card or bank information when doing transactions. However, you are grouping all of your payment methods together into one system, which could increase your exposure if someone were to hack that account.

I recommend that you only connect one or two credit cards (not all of the ones you have) to your digital wallet and do not connect any bank accounts. If you do decide to connect a bank account, ensure you are using account isolation techniques as discussed before, so that if the account is compromised they cannot get access to most of your money.

Paying with a digital wallet may affect your liability in the event of fraud. In some cases where it is possible for your wallet to hold a balance, as will PayPal, your ability to deal with fraud is based on PayPal's fraud and liability policies.

Using digital wallets is safer than using plastic credit cards today, especially since most cards are not using EMV (Chip-and-PIN) technology yet. In the end, with all factors taken into consideration, I recommend you start using a digital wallet. Although we may see a series of hacker attacks against these digital wallets, these digital wallets are here to stay, and the companies will respond accordingly to protect consumers. You can protect yourself by simply limiting how many accounts you link to your digital wallet and be aware of how you would deal with fraud or other payment issues with that digital wallet provider. There are many digital wallets so you should choose one that fits how you spend and send money. I have put together a breakdown of current digital wallets and summarized what use cases they are best suited for.

Resource: Digital wallet comparison

http://dsg.tips/wallet

In this chapter, we covered the various means – and risks – of keeping, sending, and receiving money using digital tools. In the next, we'll move to digital habits. Because, at the end of the day, do you use digital media and devices in the healthiest, most productive way for you?

SIXTEEN

LIVING IN A DIGITAL AGE

Digital Drugs

W<small>E ARE</small> living in an incredible time. We have access to one the most revolutionary communication tools mankind has ever created, the Internet, and we have marvelous devices that always keep us connected. These days, kids grow up with this technology so heavily embedded in their lives that they cannot comprehend life without it. Information and communication have never been so plentiful, and they are growing at an astounding rate.

Did you know?

▶ A survey of college students and young employees showed 33% believe the Internet is as important as air, water, food, and shelter.[57]

> 42% of men surveyed in the UK consider
> sex and Internet access to be more
> important than food or shelter.[58]

With these astonishing advancements, though, we find our
cultural and human interactions fundamentally changing,
sometimes for the worse. Many people are not even aware
of the vast quantity of television, Internet, and games they
are consuming. People use their mobile phones compulsively, sometimes to the point of addictive behavior. I do
believe there is value in entertainment; however, we have
pushed our consumption of useless information and media to an extreme. Think about how often you check email,
social networks, and the news. When given a moment of
downtime or a second waiting in line, you immediately begin "digital snacking." Often, the quality of the information
we consume is well below our mental capacities. It is written with little real reporting, few facts, and scant research
behind it. We receive barrages of useless news about celebrities and videos of animal tricks. Distraction has become a
near full-time occupation.

You don't need to consume the news or go on any
social network more than once a day, and even that isn't a
necessity. If there is information important enough for you
to know about it, your friends, family, and coworkers will
be talking about it.

Then there are those highly addictive games that we
play. These games are engineered around game theory and
use extensive testing to figure out how to lure people to
start playing, which elements grab people, which make
people play more often, and finally how they can get you

to pay for features, upgrades, bonuses, and more. Game engineers and app makers of all kinds are trying to trigger physiological and biological responses in your brain and body to hook you so that you continually want to consume their game or content.

These are all, without a doubt, digital drugs. We are addicted to them, and they manipulate us. We all use them, and we all enjoy using them. When we are made aware of these habits, we make justifications to rationalize why we indulge in them.

Are you so bored watching TV that you also have to be on your tablet at the same time? Waiting 20 seconds for an elevator is so long you have to open your phone and check it? You just read your Facebook, Twitter, and emails, and yet you pull down to refresh and check for updates so you can kill a little more time. Do you pull out your phone to avoid social interaction? Can't sit and eat alone without being on your device instead of taking in your surroundings and being present?

It's not just you, of course. Are your friends and family constantly on their phones during lunch and dinner? How about a coworker during a meeting? Have you ever seen a young couple on a date and both people are on their phones, not talking or looking at each other? I have, far too many times, and it is incredibly saddening. I challenge you to take a look around and notice the epidemic of people tied to their screens. The next time you are at a coffee shop, restaurant or walking by a bench, just take notice.

Do you feed your kids digital drugs? Is it easier to shove a tablet, phone, or computer in front of them instead of having to deal with them? Sure, this might be essential for a long ride, flight, or during a dinner in a restaurant when you want to keep them contained. But are you doing it too often? Are you creating an addiction and reliance so they can't comfortably function without it?

I grew up in front of a computer during a time when most people didn't. I first handedly had to make efforts in my life to counteract the shyness, social anxiety, and discomfort with normal social interactions that resulted. I do believe being heavily embedded in technology does have behavioral effects. I believe this will become a significantly bigger issue in the next 5 to 10 years, and psychologists will begin studying the impacts of millennials' overuse and unproductive use of technology.

How can you better yourself?

Start monitoring how often and what kind of technology you are consuming. For your desktop and laptop, there is great software that will track and help you monitor what programs you use, what websites you spend the most time on and many other aspects of your computer use. I recommend you try this out for a while, just to see if what you are actually doing lines up with what you think you are doing. Write down beforehand how much time you think you spend on social media, news, or other unproductive websites and then compare it to your real results. When you extrapolate that time spent out to a year, you might be astounded. Here is my tracking recommendation:

Resource: Track your productivity

http://dsg.tips/time

You can also use similar programs for tracking your Android phone's usage. For iOS, there isn't a great tracking app due to restrictions from Apple, but we may see improved ones in the future. See the resource above for the most up-to-date recommendation.

By monitoring your usage, you can validate how much time and attention you are or aren't wasting. From there it is easier to reduce your consumption and monitor it over time with great graphs and tracking tools: being held accountable, even to yourself, will make a difference.

Try and identify those times you compulsively look at your phone. Does it happen more in certain contexts? Are there advantages to curbing that habit? After you catch yourself doing it and notice your behavioral patterns with the phone, try to regain control. Stop using your phone anytime you are eating or hanging out with someone, for example.

 **Tip**

Try to consume only one electronic device at a time.

Try to avoid electronic devices right before bed — TV's, computers, tablets, phone, etc. They trick your body into thinking it's daytime, which suppresses melatonin, the hormone that helps your body shut down for sleep. [59]

Uninstall apps that create unhealthy or time-wasting addictions. They may include a game – perhaps even a "brain-training" game — or they might include Facebook.

By simply removing the app and consuming it on the computer instead, you will drastically reduce your need to open your phone without a purpose. Don't make excuses: just uninstall it and never open it for a couple of weeks — after a few days you won't even miss it.

Turn off alerts and push notifications for as many apps as possible, and try using airplane mode or sleep mode more often. This can prevent your technology from demanding your attention with alerts and notifications, abruptly interrupting your life. Instead, you should be opening the device when you want to consume information or communicate, not when it wants you.

Search like a pro

The Internet, and more specifically the search engines that help you find exactly what you are looking for, are one of the best tools available in modern society. The Internet is vaster than we can imagine and contains more information than any one person could absorb in a lifetime. Much of that information is of poor quality, duplicate, malicious, wrong, or manipulative. Search engines can help filter out the less valuable information. Due to the sheer amount of complex content, though, search engines can only do so much. To be an effective Internet user, you need to understand how you can use the search engine in the most efficient way — this will help you locate what you are looking for faster and with higher accuracy.

Whether you are trying to find answers to unique questions, learn a whole new skill set, do research, or find a better recipe for brownies, the following techniques will help you become a master of the search engines. When searching for something specific, you can expect it may take a few searches before you find those key documents out of the billions that surround it online.

Eliminate quickly & tabulate for in-depth research

Unless you are doing a very simple query, chances are the first result you open will not completely resolve your query. Rather than clicking the search result, open it in a new tab. You can then get predictive and open 2 or 3 of the top 10 results that look like they may answer your inquiry. As you eliminate a page, you can simply close that tab; this will leave you with the next option. Work left to right as new tabs are appended to the right, so your top result will be the first tab. As you close that tab, it will leave you with your next best tab. Finally, when you close all options, you will be left on your original search page tab. You can now quickly iterate on your search terms and repeat the process.

Using this technique can also be very helpful when one of the result tabs you opened leads to more information you want to explore. You can then open links from within that article in a new tab, the same way you did the search results. This will open the tab directly to the right of the tab you are in. You can then close your current tab and explore the additional content you just opened, or leave that tab open and browse to the next tab to the right to explore that content. This is best learned by doing: after giving it a try a few times, you'll find that the tabs are opened and ordered in a way that lend them to a quick and organized browsing experience.

I have created a video to show this technique. It is one of the most powerful research methods I use, and it is a critical one to know as you apply some of the items below.

Resource: Efficiently using tabs

`http://dsg.tips/browse`

Don't dig deep into search pages

Only in rare circumstances should you ever be leaving the first page of search results. Even beyond that, what you are looking for should be in the top 5 results. If it isn't, then chances are you need to refine your query. I'd recommend doing 3 to 5 query refinements before considering going to page two of the search results.

Ask it like a question

The easiest way to get an answer to most questions is to phrase it exactly like a question you'd ask someone in real life. "How do I…" "Where do you…" etc. Many times the search engine may attempt to extract the answer and serve it up immediately without you having to search any further. For example, try searching for "how far away is the sun" on Google. For more obscure questions, your search results will end up finding other people who may have asked this same question.

Use auto-suggest

As you type your search query, you will often see the auto-suggest box pop down. If you are having trouble finding the answer to your question or search, try using one of the auto-suggestions to phrase your query. By deleting or adding a word from your search query, you may find additional search questions.

Tip

You will find that if you delete a word in the middle of your query on Google, it will give you auto-suggestions of another word you might want to put there.

The correct terminology

In many scenarios, you may have trouble locating what you are looking for because you don't know the specialized terminology of the subject. By opening several search results and iterating your search term quickly, you should be able to find the specific keywords or terms that people are using to describe what you are looking for. Once you find a couple of those keywords, you will find it opens you up to a wealth of accurate information very quickly.

Forums

If you are looking for other people who may have had a similar experience or you'd rather see what several people are saying instead of what one person reports in an article or blog post, try adding the word "forum" to the end of the search query. This will cause forums to bubble up to the top of the results, giving you community discussions around your question. "Best way to travel Europe" and "best way to travel Europe forum" return two very different results.

Operators

There are several operators and advanced query parameters, but I'm only going to cover the ones I have found to be most useful.

The first is to exclude a keyword. If your results have a lot of noise indicating something unrelated, using exclude can help you clean that up. For example, searching for "identity thief" will produce results about the movie, Identity Thief. By adding "-movie" to the search query term, a majority of those will be removed, and that may help you find what you are looking for. The full query would read: "Identity Thief -movie".

Another important one is using quotes. Sometimes you will get too much noise, or your keywords will trigger other popular phrases. In this scenario, I recommend that you use quotes around your search term. However, you will find that putting quotes around your search term will make it significantly less flexible, and the search engine may not do things like try similar words.

Lastly, too many words may cause an issue. Sometimes just putting two of the words in quotes and the remainder outside of the quotes can help.

For a list of more operators, check out:

 **Resource:** Google search operators

http://dsg.tips/operators

Google Shortcuts

- ▶ time in <place>, time in Paris, time in New York

- ▶ define: <word>, define: theft

- ▶ Google as a calculator: 10–5 * 6^3

- ▶ Simply search for your UPS, FedEx, or USPS tracking code

- ▶ weather <location>, weather Los Angeles

You can also do conversions of many kinds, including weights and currencies. There are two formats, a simple conversion you simply type:

- ▶ kg in pounds

- ▶ USD in Euro

Or you can do specific conversions:

- ▶ 3.5 lb = ? kg

- ▶ 2 USD = ? Euro

Filters

Filters can help refine your results and are probably one of the tools I use most. Due to the vast amount of information on the Internet, you will find that many of the articles you read are outdated. By using Google's time filter, you can help keep the information showing up limited to the last hour, day, week, month, or year.

There are also advanced filters for searching a specific site, location in the world, file types, language, etc. If you need to use these, I recommend you use the advanced search page as it is much easier than trying to remember all the operators.

VS. (versus)

I often do searches with an "A vs B" format, and simply by typing in "A vs" the auto-suggestion box will indicate great ways to find other products or services that compete in that field. For example, if you were trying to choose a password manager and you only knew of 1Password, you would type, "1Password vs". On some occasions, you can even type a second vs to get even more auto-suggest results: "1Password vs vs"

Paid search results

When searching, you will often see paid search results. Paid search results are just targeted advertisements. Some people will simply ignore all ads and some people have trouble identifying which ones are the ads and which ones are the search results. Take a moment to assess if the ads you see are relevant and may be beneficial to check out. Keep in mind that these advertisements will frequently take you to a special information page about their product or service. I sometimes find it more useful to just navigate to their homepage.

Alternative search types

Don't forget that search engines provide several different category type searches. Although the default search may provide you with small snippets from these categories, it can be beneficial at times to explore a specific category. I often search only news with an additional time filter of 24 hours to dig into a recent event I want to know more about. You should use the image search feature when searching your name to see a large range of results.

Avoid unsafe places

The Internet is a vast place and full of unsafe and unfriendly places. Most people don't venture too deep into the Internet. If you mainly find websites from the top results in search engines, stick to well known websites and don't wander around to new sites often, then you are at a relatively low risk. If you have kids, click on random links, download lots of stuff, visit lots of new websites, and spend time on shady forums or clicking links on 4chan (an anonymous bulletin board filled with risky and controversial content), then you will be at a significantly higher risk. If you are going to wander the web, especially if you download random junk, use a Virtual Machine. This way if you do catch something, it won't infect your entire computer.

Validating integrity and validity of information

With online social networks, it's easier than ever for false information to spread so quickly and widely that people assume the information is real. It's so easy for a tweet that goes to thousands of people to get retweeted to millions more. Many people will retweet or share something without fact-checking it. It could be a joke, or it could be a compromised account posting misleading information. Take a moment before you contribute to this problem and disseminate information that's not grounded in solid research.

In April 2013, the Twitter feed of the Associated Press tweeted that there were explosions in the White House, and President Barack Obama had been injured. It spread incredibly fast and had over 4,000 retweets before the Associated Press was able to shut down their account — which had been hacked and used to try and spread panic on the Internet. The result was a decline in the S&P 500, wiping out an estimated $130+ billion in stock value in seconds. The market fully recovered, but the consequences of spreading false information are very real.

Sometimes this information can come from a hacked website of a news agency or a hacked Twitter account. This information could be something that's completely false, or it could come from a parody news site. A recent phenomenon on the Internet is the rise of very popular or "viral" news-parody websites. People sometimes see articles on sites like these and then immediately repost them on their social networks with a commentary, not realizing that the story was only meant to be funny. A simple Google of that website will quickly clue you into whether the story you are reading is fact or fiction. There have been multiple instances where smaller local news stations see an article from a parody website and then do a serious article or news broadcast based on the parody. People then spread that information since they heard it from a credible news outlet. It is not until the Internet has a good laugh that the misinformation gets corrected.

This also applies to the spread of "click bait" headlines or articles that are highly biased. Before spreading extremist points of view on a topic with manipulated information, perhaps check their sources and make a decision for yourself. There are many people on the Internet who will spread hate or extremist ideals without checking any of the facts.

The sheer quantity of data and information on the Internet today makes it very hard to understand what is real and what is fake. Even legitimate information is often manipulated to portray a deliberately limited side of the story by omitting a fact, taking data out of context, etc. It is extremely common for news organizations to do this — you can watch the same news points on Fox News and MSNBC and get two entirely different stories. Before disseminating information from biased sources, read the raw data. Do not allow yourself to ride the gravy train of misinformation. You will also find organizations now devoted to analyzing information with minimal bias.

Tip

The website politifact.com will rate whether statements from politicians are true or false.

Due to the economics of the Internet and advertising, more views equals more money. Even respectable news organizations have stooped to using what is known as click bait: irresistible yet misleading titles of articles that make you want to click. The problem is, the title is an exaggeration or manipulation of an article that is probably itself already exaggerated or manipulated from a true and less sensational story. The effect is much like a game of telephone. Do your part and don't spread these titles on your social networks as facts, and refrain from clicking obvious click bait titles altogether. When you do, you are perpetuating an unfortunate trend in both journalism and entertainment.

Hiding your phone number

When making certain types of phone calls, it may be beneficial for you to block your number. You can do this on a call by call basis by simply adding *67 before the number you're calling. You may also be able to turn this on for every call using one of the settings in your phone.

If you find yourself needing to give out your phone number to a dubious party, then I recommend you set up a Google Voice or similar number. This is a number that can forward calls to your existing phone, so the caller never has to know your actual number. Keep in mind, if you call them back from your regular phone and not through the Google Voice app, you may be revealing your number, so be sure to block it first. You may want to provide this phone number if you are, say, dating or selling your car on Craigslist. You may also prefer just to have a number handy that you give out any time you are required to provide a phone number outside your main community, utilities, or services. Say you make a donation and they ask for your phone number, or you enter a contest, and they require your phone number: these are all great times to hand out a Google Voice or similar number. Most features on Google Voice are completely free, so you have no excuse not to set one up and use it.

Mobile Medical ID/ICE

I recommend everyone sets up their Medical ID or ICE (In Case of Emergency) contact on their phones. These are apps or built-in features that allow some basic information to be displayed without the mobile phone being unlocked. I recommend you list your name, one or two emergency contacts, any allergies (especially to medications), your primary doctor's name and contact information. If you have health insurance, include your provider and group number. Do not include your specific subscriber number — they can locate that if needed by using your name and contacting the insurance provider; alternatively, they can get it from you after you unlock the phone and show them a picture of your health insurance card. In the event of an emergency where you are unconscious, this is important information for the EMT and hospital to have. Although this information is accessible to anyone who can hold your phone (including someone who finds or steals your phone), providing a minimal amount of critical emergency information is worth the exposure risk in my opinion.

I have put together some tutorials on setting this up and some apps you can use if you don't have the built-in Apple Medical ID feature.

Resource: Medical ID setup

`http://dsg.tips/medicalid`

Traveling

When traveling abroad, there are some things you need to think about when it comes to your electronic devices and right to privacy.

You may be subject to involuntary official review of your digital devices and data. The Harvard School of Public Health's guidance indicates, "Some foreign governments have regulations that permit the seizure of travelers' computers and the review of their contents." They may also be able to duplicate your hard drive's contents. "U.S. Customs officials are also authorized to review the contents of travelers' laptops without probable cause and can be held until your return."[60]

Using encryption to protect information, or taking encrypted data across national borders, is forbidden in some countries. Many strictly prohibit bringing new encryption technologies into the country. If your encryption product allows you to "hide" information, and those "hidden" areas can be detected, you could face criminal charges by the country's government.

Your right to privacy may not exist, depending on the country you are in — even spaces you perceive as private, like your hotel rooms, rental cars, and taxis. You may be recorded on video and audio at all times if identified by the government as a person of interest. They may follow exactly what you are doing and whom you interact with, both in person and through your electronic devices. In 2012, the State Department warned that Israeli security officials have requested access to travelers' personal email accounts and social media accounts as a condition of entry.[61]

Additionally, the government may not have the same laws and enforcement around hacking, fraud, identity theft, etc. So don't think you won't be a target just because you aren't a US government employee, an engineer with a big military defense company, or executive from a tech company; everyone is a target for criminals. This makes some foreign countries very dangerous as hackers target tourists devices. Here are some precautions you can take to avoid becoming a victim – and to stay safe from being targeted in the first place:

- ► If possible, do not take your work or personal devices with you. Use a temporary device, such as an inexpensive laptop and a prepaid "throw away" cell phone purchased specifically for travel.

- ► Minimize the data contained on the device. This is particularly true of logins and passwords, credit card information, your social security number, passport number, etc.

- ► Be sure that any device with an operating system and software is fully patched and up-to-date.

- ► When not in use, turn off the device. Do allow them to be in "sleep" or "hibernation" mode when they are not in active use.

▶ Be sure to password- or passcode-protect the device. Use unique passwords and be sure to change them as soon as you return to the United States.

▶ Assume that anything you do on the device, particularly over the Internet, will be intercepted. In some cases, encrypted data may be decrypted. This means you should not log into any account you don't absolutely have to. Any account you do log into should have the password changed when you return to the United States.

▶ Keep the device with you at all times during your travel. Do not assume it will be safe in your hotel room or even in a hotel safe.

▶ Upon returning from your travels, immediately discontinue use of the device. The hard drive of the device should be reformatted, and the operating system and other related software reinstalled, or the device properly disposed of.

▶ Change any and all passwords you may have used abroad.

▶ Tape over any integrated laptop cameras.

▶ Physically disconnect any integrated laptop microphones if possible.

▶ Install a privacy screen on your laptop to discourage "shoulder surfing."

▶ Disable all file sharing.

▶ Disable all unnecessary network protocols (e.g., wifi, Bluetooth, infrared, etc.)

- ▶ Backup any data you may have stored on the device.

- ▶ If you need to send and receive email while traveling, create a temporary "throwaway" account on Gmail, Yahoo Mail or a similar service before you travel.

- ▶ Limit or avoid making or receiving voice calls, using voicemail, instant messaging, text messaging, and using faxes.[62]

It is forbidden to leave the United States with any encrypted device (laptop, phone, external drive, or electronic media of any kind) if you are traveling to Cuba, Iran, North Korea, Sudan or Syria. The following countries do not allow you to enter with an encrypted device (or you have to apply for a license ahead of time): Belarus, Burma, China, Hungary, Iran, Kazakhstan, Moldova, Morocco, Russia, Saudi Arabia, Tunisia, and Ukraine.

Many countries support the Wassenaar Arrangement, which allows you to enter a country, use and leave with encrypted data and encryption software, as long as you do not create, enhance, share, sell, or otherwise distribute the encryption technology while visiting the country. These countries include: Argentina, Australia, Austria, Belgium, Bulgaria, Canada, Croatia, Czech Republic, Denmark, Estonia, Finland, France, Germany, Greece, Hungary, Ireland, Italy, Japan, Latvia, Lithuania, Luxembourg, Malta, Netherlands, New Zealand, Norway, Poland, Portugal, Republic of Korea, Romania, Slovakia, Slovenia, South Africa, Spain, Sweden, Switzerland, Turkey, United Kingdom, and the United States.[63]

Many people traveling to China and similar countries will buy a throwaway phone and laptop due to the increase in corporate espionage there, the large community of skilled hackers, and the government's blind eye to much of it. If you work for a company, ask them for a temporary laptop to take with you — they will probably oblige.

Beyond just worrying about your electronic devices and their encryption, you should also leave unneeded car keys, house keys, smart cards, credit/debit cards, security badges, and key fobs at home.

 **Tip**

Notify your banks about the cards you plan to take with you and what dates you will be there. This will prevent them from automatically blocking transactions they believe are fraudulent, and it will help prevent fraud if your card is stolen while you are traveling.

You should also make copies of your key documents: passport, foreign visa, hotel confirmation, airline ticket, driver's license, credit cards, and traveler's check serial numbers you plan to take on the trip. As you are keeping these separate from your main copies, you are increasing your risk that someone can get hold of them if they steal one of your two storage locations. Because of this, I personally keep pictures of all these items on my cell phone, encrypted with a password. Another good option is to upload the pictures to a cloud platform that you can access from any computer, like Dropbox. Be sure to delete them after your trip!

Should you decide to take your primary phone to another country, I recommend you clean up and remove as much extra data as you can, including pictures, notes, apps, etc.

 Resource: Traveling guide

`http://dsg.tips/travel`

Copyright of digital goods

Most things that an individual creates on the Internet are protected by copyright laws. This includes but is not limited to books, music, pictures, films, computer programs, and advertisements. Keep in mind that when you post content on different services, you may be signing away some of your rights. By uploading a picture, that service may retain the right to use your picture however they want. Most businesses aren't in the business of stealing their customers photos for their own gain, but there could be some instances where they use your data and it would not be in your best interest. You also have to be sure not to infringe on other people's copyright. Downloading content illegally is one of the largest offenders. If you are familiar with torrents and download torrents of any kind, you should read my article on how to protect yourself:

Resource: How to torrent safely

`http://dsg.tips/torrent`

Although you will automatically own the copyright of any images or material you create, you often give away many of those rights when you upload them to websites and social networks. This was discussed in the social networks section, and you may want to review that if you intend to share professional work online.

Becoming anonymous

There are different levels of anonymity online that you may be interested in achieving. The more you want to increase your anonymity online, the more inconvenient using the Internet will be. Because of this, most people decide they don't really care. However, I have put together articles and directions for different levels of interest.

If you want to take a minimal level of caution while keeping the convenience factor and slightly increasing your privacy, see the beginner article:

Resource: Increase online privacy

`http://dsg.tips/minprivacy`

If you want to get significantly more anonymous using tools like a VPN or Tor, check out my intermediate article:

Resource: VPN recommendations

`http://dsg.tips/bitcoin`

If you are interested in setting up a completely anonymous identity on the Internet and wandering into the Dark Web, check out my advanced, in-depth article:

Resource:
Becoming anonymous online

`http://dsg.tips/darkweb`

Bitcoin

Bitcoin, a cryptocurrency launched in 2009, is a recent and rapidly growing breakthrough, essentially, a decentralized virtual currency and transaction system. The reason bitcoin is unique is that there is no central authority, like a bank, that runs it. It is a decentralized peer-to-peer system that is fully owned and run by the people.

Every transaction on the bitcoin network is stored in a public ledger that is available for anyone to view. Despite that, you can still achieve privacy as your wallet is not directly tied to your identity. However, this does not make it anonymous, as when you pay for something and provide your shipping details, that address can then be associated to you by the other party. There are also ways to trace your bitcoin wallet to your real identity through the regulated exchange you use to purchase bitcoins using USD. However, there are ways to make that money less traceable and connected to your identity if you wished to do so. I cover this in my advanced article on becoming anonymous.

So what makes bitcoin so awesome besides the ability to have money in a James Bond-style untraceable account in the digital world? For one, because it is not centrally controlled, you can send money anywhere in the world, anytime. The "bank" is never closed, there are no cross-border regulations or delays, nor any bureaucracy of any kind. Additionally, there are no fees to receive bitcoins and a tiny small fee to send them. It is not a percentage-based fee structure like the expensive payment processing we currently use. Other pro's include:

- ► It isn't subject to inflation like currencies like the US Dollar.

- ► It can add privacy to your banking and transactions if you want it to.

- ► It is very hard for a central authority like the government or IRS to take away your money.

So what is the downside? Bitcoin is still a bit volatile but has significantly stabilized in the first half of 2015. It is more risky to use than USD at this time, because of these value fluctuations. But we hope over time this will change. With the increased adoption of bitcoin, we are getting closer and closer to a mass adoption. I wouldn't recommend you invest all your money into bitcoins, but if you have some money to play with, you might want to check it out. It may come into more common use in the next few years as a common way of sending each other money.

For more resources about bitcoins and how to safely get started with acquiring and using them, I have put together some great resources for you here:

Resource: More about Bitcoins

http://dsg.tips/bitcoin

Buying a new car

Why are we talking about buying a car in a technology book? Well, simply put, almost every chapter will directly apply to the pre-, mid-, and post-purchase process of buying a car. Not only that, but I will cover how to use technology to help you get the best possible price and feel confident throughout the process. You could consider this a practical application of many of the items discussed in this book.

Do a credit check on yourself and sign up for credit monitoring. This is the first step, because if there is any fraud on your credit report, it will stop the entire process of buying a car dead in its tracks. Best to do this weeks ahead of time so you can deal with any surprises. Don't forget: you will want your credit use percentage as low as possible during this process, and it can take weeks for that to be reflected in your report. Keep the credit report monitoring through your buying process. This will ensure if any fraud pops up during the process you can quickly fix it, or if anyone runs your credit without your permission, you will be notified.

Determine what you want to buy: exact car, model, color, options, etc. You can always test drive at the dealership, but it may be a hassle dealing with them. Never give them contact details to do a test drive other than your driver's license. And never give them your keys. If they try to prevent giving you your license back while attempting to get more info out of you, escalate to management immediately or threaten a bad Yelp review. To avoid being put in any of these situations, I recommend you try and find a place that rents the car you are interested in buying. Two or three days driving the car will give you significantly more understanding of whether the car is right for you.

Pick the right time to buy. You will always have an advantage if they are trying to move inventory near the end of the quarter, end of the year or when trying to make room for the arrival of new models. Take into account that it may be a couple-week-long process, so plan ahead; don't start on the last day of the year.

Check your DMV and CLUE report before applying for insurance to ensure there are no surprises, bad information, or something that might be about to fall off (like a speeding ticket) that would make you wait a tad bit longer before starting the process.

- ► Get your junk phone number and email set up.

- ► Get the most value of your used car

- ► Check the Carfax report on your car if you are going to sell or trade it in.

- ► Do market research, on Kelley Blue Book, Craigslist, and other vendors.

- ► List your car on Craigslist with your junk phone number and measure the response at different price points.

I recommend you target selling to a private party on or directly after a pay day. The price will probably be more from a private party, but a dealer will take a significant amount of hassle out of the process. You can have them give you an offer after your car purchase has been fully negotiated. Then negotiate the price upward as high as you can get them, or to a level you would be comfortable with.

Shop for insurance before purchasing, as you will want to calculate that into what this car will cost you monthly. Use your junk info and shop several sites — they don't run your credit so you shouldn't need to provide your social

You may want to finance on your own. Don't run your credit too many times; try to shop without running credit; when getting pre-approved, ask if they can do so without a hard credit inquiry.

Use edmunds.com and searches on the Internet to find the MSRP and invoice price for the car.

Use online sites to get quotes from bulk dealers and negotiated websites. Some examples are CarsDirect.com, TrueCar.com, Overstock.com, Costco.com, and Zag.com.

Find any manufacturer incentives, discounts, or rebates that you may be able to use. Because these are paid to the dealership from the manufacturer, it should have no impact on your negotiated price. Don't bring these up until the end, after you negotiated a price. You can find these by checking the manufactures website or searching car forums.

Understand any dealership special offers like cash back or rebate money.

Based on your research, you will probably get a quote from several local dealerships. Expand your reach to as far as you are willing to travel and contact the Internet sales of every dealership in that area that you don't already have a quote from (using TrueCar or similar). Ensure to ask them to show ALL the fees so you can be sure you are getting the best number.

You now have the lowest offer directly from the dealerships or from your TrueCar (or similar) research. Reach out to the other dealers, tell them you have a dealership willing to sell it for $X (your lowest offer), and ask them if they can do any better.

You may find that the car you want with the color and options is only available at a couple of dealerships. This means other dealerships quoting you are having to incur the cost of shipping that car over to their dealership. I recommend you visit a dealership and just ask them to see what kind of inventory would be available if you were interested in buying. The dealerships who don't have to pay for a transfer will most likely have the most negotiating flexibility.

You should also identify the dealerships that sell the most cars. A dealership that moves more cars can afford to make less per car and may also get additional kickbacks from the manufacturer for being a high-volume seller.

Remember

Factors including the amount of available inventory, how new the car is, and what the demand for the car is will greatly determine your negotiating power.

If the car is in high demand and there are very few that meet the color and options you want, you will have a hard time negotiating the price down. If your car is popular and every dealership has one with the options you want, you have a lot of negotiating power.

Don't play the game of negotiating what monthly price you want to pay. Stick to the price and try to drive it as close to invoice, if not below as you can. Don't believe they aren't making money if you get the car at or below invoice. They still get paid a percentage from the manufacturer after the sale, and it isn't your problem. After that, apply your manufacturer discounts and rebates. By researching ahead of time, you may be able to get discounts and rebates by signing up for a car club or something similar.

Negotiating online will make things a lot easier, but you will inevitably have to see them face to face to finish up the deal. If they change the terms on you at all or won't go to a price that you want, simply walk away from the deal. Walking away is hard, but that is how they get you. They will use lines like, "Are you really willing to lose this deal for a couple of hundred bucks?" .

Check out the car forums —many people will have posted what price they paid and where.

When done correctly, research and due diligence can save you thousands when buying your new car and can limit many of the uncertainties involved.

The dealership will run your credit two different times; this is very common, but try and avoid it if possible. If you have financing already, they shouldn't need to run it a second time. The first time is just to validate your identity, which they legally need to do to sell you a car. Do not give them your social security number until the car is negotiated and agreed upon and you are ready to sign. They will try and get it early to prequalify you, which will probably result in a hard inquiry on your credit and a decreased credit score. This is a big mistake as you may not end up buying from that specific dealership.

Also, beware of dealerships or loan companies that offer to get you the best rate by shopping you across a dozen lenders. Each lender will do a credit hit, and your score will take a major drop overnight.

After buying the car, you will receive junk offers in the mail for years. Some of these will look like legitimate extensions of your warranty but are just an advertisement from some other company. They will have a surprising amount of information about you and your car, though. Don't be lured in.

Increasing Productivity

I have collected and refined many tools and techniques I use for achieving very high productivity when using technology. Because this is such a detailed and dynamic piece of content, it did not fit neatly into the pages of this book, and I recommend you check out the productivity series on my website:

Resource: Productivity tips

http://dsg.tips/productivity

This chapter covered a wide range of topics, all important to the way we live now. Just because distraction is always at our fingertips does not mean we have to give up on efficiency, adventure, and mindfulness. In the next chapter, we'll turn to the last part of the guide, and hopefully one you won't have to consult too often: what to do when you have been a victim of cybercrime.

SEVENTEEN

HANDLING FRAUD

What to do when you have been victimized

R EGARDLESS OF the precautions we take, sometimes attacks still succeed. They can sting, both financially and psychologically. Being victimized might mean that you cannot pay your bills on time because stolen money might not be refunded in time. This is also why it is important to establish a police report, call the companies with whom you have any outstanding bills, and act quickly and proactively. Many people will wait until it is a problem and a bill is past due before calling and trying to explain the situation. You will find companies and service providers to be much more accommodating if you reach out early to explain your possible upcoming concern.

No matter what type of theft or fraud you are victim to, keep a detailed log of events. Places you called and what time, who you spoke with, and any report or incident numbers associated with the call should all be in that log. It may come in handy further down the road. This data can also be useful for security researchers looking for a better understanding of what people go through.

Keep a list

You should keep a list of all your account numbers, expiration dates, customer service phone numbers, etc. Keep them somewhere safe in your home — hidden away or ideally inside a safe. This is good to have, in case your wallet is stolen. If you think about it, are you really prepared if you were to lose your wallet or got hit by some form of identity theft? The aftermath of these events can be incredibly stressful, and being organized and prepared can make the ordeal significantly easier.

I recommended earlier that you add a contact on your cell phone for each credit card or bank card that you keep in your wallet. This way you can easily contact them if lost or stolen. Do not include the account numbers or other sensitive information. However, having that at home in a safe place can come in handy. I recommend you keep it encrypted on a thumb drive. Your auto and health insurance numbers can be kept on your phone using a picture or notes, but another identifying information is best not on your phone. Do you know your driver's license number and license plate number, for example? Keep those written down somewhere safe.

Wallet

The most important thing to do when your wallet is lost or stolen is to act quickly. Here is what I recommend you do:

Call your bank and credit card providers for the cards that were in your wallet. Calling before the card is used for a fraudulent transaction will keep your liability to zero. Waiting to call can increase your liability. To be clear, you are not canceling or closing your account; they will just deactivate your current card and provide you with a new number.

File a police report to establish a record of your loss. This is not so they will send out the troops to find it — instead, this is to protect you in the event you become the victim of identity theft. List the items that were in your wallet and request a copy of the report as you may need it later.

Call all three credit bureaus and put a fraud alert on your account. There is a 90-day protection policy for events just like this.

Call the DMV and report your license as lost or stolen. They can place a flag on your account and will issue you a replacement card.

If you kept your health insurance card with you, call your insurer and alert them to the theft. Ask them to change your account number. Same deal if you kept your auto insurance in your wallet.

Credit & Debit Card

Fraudulent use of your credit card is going to be the most prevalent follow-up event to a theft. As soon as you notice the fraudulent transaction, simply contact that provider and alert them. They will disable your current card and issue a new one. As long as you do not see transactions on your other credit cards or changes in your credit report, then this was probably a straightforward case. You can update your credit card information for recurring payments and get on with your life. If you have your credit card number stolen continually, there is probably a skimmer somewhere that you frequent. Look at your transaction history to see if you can identify places you used it every time before it was stolen. You can then bring it to the attention of that establishment's owner and law enforcement. You may also want to avoid that establishment.

After you receive your replacement card, take a look at the previous month's statement and identify all the recurring charges. Using that list, you will conveniently know what accounts you need to update.

Identity Theft

If you begin to experience signs of more serious identity theft, then things are not as straightforward. Since this can manifest itself in many different ways, you will have to handle it on a case by case basis. It is notably more serious anytime someone uses your social security number, opens an account under your name, or gains access to your accounts. Once you suspect it, do a full check of all your accounts, credit reports, and other digital reputation systems covered in this book. These are the general steps you should follow in all cases:

- ► Contact any companies involved with the fraud and alert them of the situation.

- ► Place a fraud alert on all your accounts and pull all three of your credit reports.

- ► Report the theft or fraud to the FTC here: https://www.ftc.gov/complaint

- ► File a report with your local police department and get a copy of the report.

For more details on how to handle all forms of identity theft, there is a great government resource to walk you through what to do. Check it out here:

 Resource: IdentityTheft.gov

https://www.identitytheft.gov/

Online accounts

The key to recovering most online accounts quickly is having properly set up the security recovery features on your account to begin with. This means having an up-to-date email, phone number, and any other applicable information. Sometimes your name and birthday may also be used to validate the account — keep that in mind before you fill out fake information. You should also ensure your forgot password questions are up-to-date, and you know the answers to all of them. Some websites even allow for a secondary email and backup phone number on the account.

In the event your account is compromised, the intruder will probably try and change all of these things to prevent you from regaining access to the account. Unless they have access to your secondary email, though, you usually have 24 or 72 hours to cancel an email change by clicking a link that will be sent to your account. If you receive one of these emails, you should change your password and completely reset everything in your account.

Remember

If you get an email for a forgot password or failed login attempt, then someone may be poking around trying to get into your account. This isn't necessarily always malicious, it may just be someone who has a similar username and forgot theirs.

Most online accounts are easy to recover as it is obvious when one has been compromised; however it may take varying periods of time, depending on the service provider. If you can't recover the account by following the "forgot password" dialog, then you will need to open a support ticket or go through a flow for account recovery. It should be fairly easy to locate this on the help or contact section of the service provider.

In this chapter, we went through a narrative of how your reactions to a cyber theft would ideally play out. In the next, we'll come full circle: the book concludes with a call to action and a comprehensive list of everything you can do to pre-empt cybercrime in the first place.

EIGHTEEN

Digital Chores

W E HAVE covered a lot of material in this book. Congratulations on making it almost all the way through! But it will only help you if you take action. Although I wish we could all be security experts, my goal is to get you to commit to the minimal amount of effort that will make you significantly more secure.

Remember

You undoubtedly have chores in many aspects of your life, and keeping your digital identity and data safe and secure needs to become one of them.

I expect this will take you 1 to 3 hours, once a month, and one full day once a year at a minimum. When you take into account the possible consequences of not doing this, it is clearly time well spent. I find it best to set up a recurring event on your calendar for your monthly and yearly to-do's. After you become comfortable doing these chores, you may find it significantly easier to ramp up your security commitment. To get a digital, printable, up-to-date version of the following checklist, check out this resource:

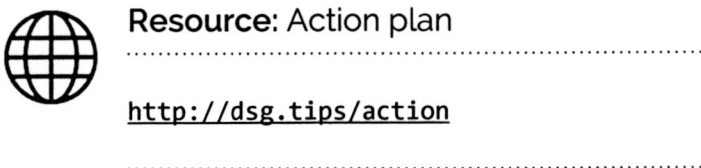

Resource: Action plan

http://dsg.tips/action

Right now

► Do you have back-ups and disaster recovery in place? Ensure you are following the 3-2-1 backup rule.

► Do you have passwords and encryption on all your devices?

► Opt out of prescreened credit card offers and mailing lists, and enroll in the Do Not Call Registry.

► Enable automatic updates for your phone, laptop/desktop, browser, and anti-virus software, and make sure they are up-to-date

► Check your privacy settings on all of your social networks.

► Enable two-factor authentication on email, cloud, backup and all financial accounts.

► Search the Internet and identify public information about yourself — then scrub it.

► Audit your wallet to remove things you shouldn't have in there.

Monthly

► Check credit card and bank statements for unusual activity.

► Take backup offline if you deem necessary.

► Ensure your online backup is working as expected.

► Ensure virus scan, browsers, operating systems, and cell phone software are all up to date — you shouldn't have to watch this as closely because you should be using automatic update. After ensuring the automatic update is working, simply make sure quarterly auto-update is still enabled and working as expected.

► Scanning paper documents and shred those that can be thrown away.

Quarterly

► Validate auto-update is enabled and has been working for your browsers, operating systems, and cell phone.

► Check your phone and computer tracking is working properly and properly secured.

► If you have credit monitoring, which you should, pull an updated report and give it a quick check.

Yearly

- ► Change your passwords.

- ► Search the Internet for yourself and check for anything new or unexpected.

- ► Check public information websites if you aren't using an automated tool to do so.

- ► Check and update your privacy settings on all your social networks.

- ► Check your wireless router firmware version and update it.

- ► Check your free credit report.

- ► Do you need to increase your credit card limit to lower your monthly utilization and increase your credit score? If so, do it.

- ► Pull your bank reputation, DMV, and insurance systems records.

- ► Check your socialsecurity.gov account for unexpected income being declared under your name.

- ► If you don't do regular offline backups, do one at least once a year. Buy a thumb drive or external hard drive. Don't risk losing years of pictures and documents. If you rely on online-only backups, a hacker could wipe you out completely.

- ► Feeling courageous? Format your computer and reinstall your applications, resync/restore your data from your backup source. It is a good exercise of your disaster recovery plan and will help ensure your computer is running optimally and malware-free.

► Check your forgot password questions, account backup/recovery methods (email and phone numbers), etc.

Ongoing

▶ Are you introducing new electronic devices into your life/household? Ensure the software and firmware are up to date. Do some quick searches online to ensure there are no security issues, recalls, or other important complaints about that product on the Internet.

▶ Be on the lookout for suspicious alerts (both legitimate and illegitimate) about your accounts

Thank you

Thank you for reading, and I hope you truly enjoyed this book. If you found value in this book, please share and help spread the word about the Digital Survival Guide. This small action makes a big difference, and I greatly appreciate your support. Let's help make the Internet a safer place together!

http://dsg.tips/share

Please leave a review on Amazon, your blog or email me your feedback. Your opinion not only affects other readers' purchasing decisions, but it matters to me as well. Only with your feedback can I make the book better! Please reach out by visiting:

http://dsg.tips/feedback

To stay in touch and get the most recent news and updates, visit the website:

https://digitalsurvivalguide.net

Thank you for reading, and be safe out there my friends!

Endnotes

1. Javelin Strategy & Research: 2015 IDENTITY FRAUD: Protecting Vulnerable Populations. https://www.javelinstrategy.com/coverage-area/2015-identity-fraud-protecting-vulnerable-populations

2. "2015 Identity Fraud: Protecting Vulnerable Populations," Javelin Strategy & Research, 2015, https://www.javelinstrategy.com/coverage-area/2015-identity-fraud-protecting-vulnerable-populations

3. "Identity Theft Report," Federal Trade Commission, 2003, https://www.ftc.gov/sites/default/files/documents/reports/federal-trade-commission-identity-theft-program/synovatereport.pdf

4. Carly Okle, "Password Statistics," Entrepreneur, June 2015, http://www.entrepreneur.com/article/246902

5. "Press Release," Treasury Inspector General for Tax Administration,April 2015, https://www.treasury.gov/tigta/press/press_tigta-2015-08.htm

6. Amanda Hahn and Chris Holmes, "The 8 Creepiest Cases of Identity Theft of All Time," September 2012, http://www.cracked.com/article_19973_the-8-creepiest-cases-identity-theft-all-time_p2.html

7. "Apple Media Advisory," September 2014, http://www.apple.com/pr/library/2014/09/02Apple-Media-Advisory.html

8. "Wifi Networks Security," graphs.com, May 2012, http://graphs.net/wifi-stats.html

9. Jamie Condliffe, "The Top 25 Most Popular Passwords of 2014," Gizmodo, January 2015, http://gizmodo.com/the-25-most-popular-passwords-of-2014-were-all-doomed-1680596951

10. Trustwave Global Security Report, 2015, https://www2.trustwave.com/rs/815-RFM-693/images/2015_TrustwaveGlobalSecurityReport.pdf

11. "How Secure Is My Password?," Small Hadron Collider, 2009-2014, https://howsecureismypassword.net/

12. Mat Honan, "How Apple and Amazon Security Leaks Led to My Epic Hacking," Wired, August 2012, http://www.wired.com/2012/08/apple-amazon-mat-honan-hacking/

13. "PIN Analysis," DataGenetics, 2009-2013, http://www.datagenetics.com/blog/september32012/

14. Dan Terzian, "The Fifth Amendment, Encryption, and the Forgotten State Interest, UCLA Law Review, 2015, http://www.uclalawreview.org/the-fifth-amendment-encryption-and-the-forgotten-state-interest/

15. Hanni Fakhoury and Nadia Kayyali, "Know Your Rights," The Electronic Frontier Foundation, October 2014, https://www.eff.org/issues/know-your-rights

16. John Hutchins, "Do Email Disclaimers Really Work?", American Bar Association, February 2013, http://apps.americanbar.org/litigation/committees/technology/articles/winter2013-0213-do-email-disclaimers-really-work.html

17. "Our Mission," Facebook Newsroom, 2015, http://newsroom.fb.com/company-info/

18. "Tell Your Stories Here," Twitter, 2015, https://about.twitter.com/company

19. "About Us," LinkedIn, 2015, https://press.linkedin.com/about-linkedin

20. Gemma Mullin, "Woman has £380 horse race winnings STOLEN after posting betting slip on Facebook, Mirror, November 2015, http://www.mirror.co.uk/news/world-news/woman-380-horse-race-winnings-6767748

21. "Keys Can be Copied from Afar, Jacobs School Computer Scientists Show," October 2008, http://www.jacobsschool.ucsd.edu/news/news_releases/release.sfe?id=791

22. "2012 State of Mobile Etiquette & Digital Sharing," Intel Newsroom, 2012, http://newsroom.intel.com/servlet/JiveServlet/showImage/2420/infographic_02_sm.jpg

23. "Avoiding Social Engineering and Phishing Attacks," US-CERT, October 2009, https://www.us-cert.gov/ncas/tips/ST04-014

24. Stacy Cowley, "How a lying 'social engineer' hacked Wal-Mart," CNN, August 2012, http://money.cnn.com/2012/08/07/technology/walmart-hack-defcon/

25. Angela Hennessy, "We Spoke to a Social Engineer About How He Hacks People and Infiltrates 'Secure' Companies," VICE, July 2013, https://www.vice.com/en_ca/read/we-spoke-to-a-social-engineer-about-how-he-hacks-people-and-infiltrates-secure-companies

26. "State of Phone Fraud Report," Pindrop Security, 2014-2015, http://www.pindropsecurity.com/phone-fraud-report/

27. Doug Shadel and David Dudley, " 'Are You Real?' – Inside an Online Dating Scam," AARP, June/July 2015, http://www.aarp.org/money/scams-fraud/info-2015/online-dating-scam.html

28. Brian Fraga, "Swansea police pay $750 'ransom' after computer virus strikes," Herald News, November 2013, http://www.heraldnews.com/article/20131115/NEWS/311159409 and Gregory Pratt, "Midlothian cops pay ransom to retrieve data from hacker," Chicago Tribune, February 2015, http://www.chicagotribune.com/news/local/breaking/ct-midlothian-hacker-ransom-met-20150220-story.html

29. "True Phishing Stories," University of Florida, http://sarasota.ifas.ufl.edu/FCS/phish_stories.pdf

30. "Spam and Phishing in Q1," Kaspersky Lab, May 2015, http://www.kaspersky.com/about/news/virus/2015/Spam-and-Phishing-in-Q1-New-domains-revitalize-old-spam

31. "iOS6: Understanding Location Services," Apple, February 2015, support.apple.com/en-us/HT5467

32. "Wifi Networks Security," graphs.com, May 2012, http://graphs.net/wifi-stats.html

33. "Vulnerability Statistics," CVE Details, 2015, http://www.cvedetails.com/product/6761/Adobe-Flash-Player.html?vendor_id=53

34. Ariel Sanchez, "Personal banking apps leak through phone," IOActive Labs, January 2014, http://blog.ioactive.com/2014/01/personal-banking-apps-leak-info-through.html

35. Michael Zhang, "Photographer Loses Pictures from 20+ Shoots After Car Broken Into," PetaPixel, September 2015, http://petapixel.com/2015/09/10/photographer-loses-pictures-from-20-shoots-after-car-broken-into/

36. "OS X Mountain Lion: Prevent deleted files from being read," Apple, October 2015, https://support.apple.com/kb/PH11124?locale=en_US

37. Jack Doyle, "Invasion of the pickpockets," Daily Mail, July 2012, http://www.dailymail.co.uk/news/article-2175867/London-Olympics-2012-As-1-700-fall-victim-pickpockets-day-Eastern-European-gangs-it.html and
Anil Dawar, "1,600 victims a day of street crime," Express, October 2012, http://www.express.co.uk/news/uk/352948/1-600-victims-a-day-of-street-crime

38. "Living a Lie," The FBI, October 2012, https://www.fbi.gov/news/stories/2012/october/identity-theft-that-lasted-decades

39. "Is the Internet a fundamental human necessity?", Cisco Connected World Technology Report, 2011, "Is the Internet a fundamental human necessity?", Cisco Connected World Technology Report, 2011, http://www.cisco.com/c/en/us/solutions/enterprise/connected-world-technology-report/index.html#~2011,

40. Laura Shin, " 'Someone Had Taken Over My Life,'" Forbes, November 2014, http://www.forbes.com/sites/laurashin/2014/11/18/someone-had-taken-over-my-life-an-identity-theft-victims-story/

41. Amanda Hahn and Chris Holmes, "The 8 Creepiest Cases of Identity Theft of All Time," September 2012, http://www.cracked.com/article_19973_the-8-creepiest-cases-identity-theft-all-time_p2.html

42. Amanda Hahn and Chris Holmes, "The 8 Creepiest Cases of Identity Theft of All Time," September 2012, http://www.cracked.com/article_19973_the-8-creepiest-cases-identity-theft-all-time.html

43. "Consumers and Mobile Financial Services 2014," Board of Governors of the Federal Reserve System, March 2014, http://www.federalreserve.gov/econresdata/consumers-and-mobile-financial-services-report-201403.pdf

44. "Juice Jacking," Wall of Sheep, 2015 http://www.wallofsheep.com/pages/juice; and Justin Rocket Silverman, "Internet viruses charge ahead, at public power stations," New York Daily News, August 2013, http://m.nydailynews.com/life-style/Internet-viruses-charge-public-power-stations-article-1.1422680; and Gary Davis, "US-B Careful," McAfee Consumer Blog, November 2013, https://blogs.mcafee.com/consumer/public-iphone-chargers-malware

45. Darlene Storm, "Hacker hijacks wireless Foscam baby monitor, talks and freaks out nanny," Computer World, February 2015, http://www.computerworld.com/article/2878741/hacker-hijacks-wireless-foscam-baby-monitor-talks-and-freaks-out-nanny.html

46. HackersOnBoard, "Black Hat 2013 – Exploiting Network Surveillance Cameras Like a Hollywood Hacker," November 2013, https://www.youtube.com/watch?v=B8DjTcANBx0

47. Alex Goldman, "When Going Online Will Send You To Prison," dig, April 2015, http://digg.com/2015/when-going-online-will-send-you-to-prison

48. Cheryl Rodewig, "Geotagging poses security risks," United States Army, March 2012, http://www.army.mil/article/75165/Geotagging_poses_security_risks/

49. "Examples of Identity Theft Investigations – Fiscal Year 2015," IRS, 2015, https://www.irs.gov/uac/Examples-of-Identity-Theft-Investigations-Fiscal-Year-2015

50. "Examples of Identity Theft Investigations – Fiscal Year 2015," IRS, 2015, https://www.irs.gov/uac/Examples-of-Identity-Theft-Investigations-Fiscal-Year-2015

51. "How long with negative information remain on my credit report?" myFICO, http://www.myfico.com/crediteducation/questions/Negative-Items-On-Credit-Report-Chapter-7-13.aspx

52. "How Long Does Information Stay on My Credit Report?" Equifax Experts, September 2013, http://blog.equifax.com/credit/how-long-does-information-stay-on-my-credit-report/#

53. Ayaz Nanji, "An Identity Theft Nightmare," CBS News, February 2005, http://www.cbsnews.com/news/an-identity-theft-nightmare/

54. Amanda Hahn and Chris Holmes, "The 8 Creepiest Cases of Identity Theft of All Time," September 2012, http://www.cracked.com/article_19973_the-8-creepiest-cases-identity-theft-all-time.html

55. "Tech Firm Ubiquiti Suffers $46M Cyberheist," Krebs on Security, August 2015, http://krebsonsecurity.com/2015/08/tech-firm-ubiquiti-suffers-46m-cyberheist/

56. "Credit or Debit Card Surcharge State Statutes," NCSL, October 2015, http://www.ncsl.org/research/financial-services-and-commerce/credit-or-debit-card-surcharges-statutes.aspx

57. "Is the Internet a fundamental human necessity?", Cisco Connected World Technology Report, 2011, http://www.cisco.com/c/en/us/solutions/enterprise/connected-world-technology-report/index.html#~2011,

58. Ian Barker, "Sex and internet rank above food and shelter for 42 percent of UK men," betanews, 2012, http://betanews.com/2013/06/18/sex-and-internet-rank-above-food-and-shelter-for-42-percent-of-uk-men/

59. Lighting Research Center, Rensselaer Polytechnic Institute, "The impact of light from computer monitors on melatonin levels in college students." December 2011 http://www.ncbi.nlm.nih.gov/pubmed/21552190

60. "International Travel: Electronic Devices and Encryption Software," Hard T.H. Chan School of Public Health, http://www.hsph.harvard.edu/export-controls/international-travel-electronic-devices-and-encryption-software/

61. "Travel Warning – Israel, the West Bank, and Gaza," Embassy of the United States – Cotonou – Benin," August 2012, http://cotonou.usembassy.gov/en-twisrael081112.html

62. "Cyber Security Tips for Traveling Abroad with Mobile Electronic Devices," North Dakota State University, https://www.ndsu.edu/its/security/traveling_abroad_with_electronic_devices/

63. "The Wassenaar Arrangement," December 2015, http://www.wassenaar.org/introduction/index.html

Index

CPSIA information can be obtained
at www.ICGtesting.com
Printed in the USA
FSOW01n0533160216
16968FS

9 780997 213799